PREMIERSHIP GROUNDS

EVERY CLUB AND EVERY GROUND SINCE 1992

PREMIERSHIP GROUNDS

EVERY CLUB AND EVERY GROUND SINCE 1992

CLAIRE WELCH AND IAN WELCH

FORWARD BY **LAWRIE SANCHEZ**

COMPENDIUM

This edition published in 2008 by

COMPENDIUM

ISBN 978-1-906347-12-3

© 2008 Compendium Publishing,
43 Frith Street, Soho, London, W1D 4SA, United Kingdom

Cataloging-in-Publication data is available from the
Library of Congress

Printed and bound in China

Design: Peran Publishing Services

PREVIOUS PAGE: *Chelsea celebrate winning the Premier League title
in May 2005.*

RIGHT: *No other club has won the Premiership title as many times as
Manchester United.*

CONTENTS

FOREWORD

I know it's a cliché that has been quoted many times before by so many people – both players and managers alike – but I can confirm that the Premiership is without doubt the best league in the world. It attracts top foreign players who come to show off their talents at some of the best stadiums that the game has to offer.

This book covers every club who has played in the Premiership since its inception in the 1992-93 season. It might perhaps be surprising to many of you that there have been 40 teams who have made it to the top of the pyramid – almost half the clubs in the four professional divisions – but, due to the fact that many of them have been forced to relocate to new purpose-built stadia because of the geographical restrictions imposed on their existing locations, far more grounds have witnessed the highs and lows of Premiership football than that number. This will only increase as teams such as Liverpool, Everton and Portsmouth among others have all put forward suggestions for new sites in recent years. While many fans are obviously dismayed that their beloved clubs leave their historical home, they can be reassured that the new stadium will be state of the art and hungry for success.

My professional playing career began in 1978. I was privileged to play for three of the teams covered in this book, and I have been lucky enough to have visited the majority of the grounds included in these pages. I started as a youngster with Reading and then moved to Wimbledon at a time when the "Crazy Gang" were reaching the pinnacle of their achievements before transferring to Swindon Town in time for their initiation into Premiership football. I have also managed Fulham and would relish the opportunity to take the helm at another Premiership club.

Enjoy this book as it takes you on a trip down memory lane and relive the excitement and thrills that the Premiership has brought us so far!

Lawrie Sanchez

LEFT: *A moment of glory: Lawrie Sanchez is surrounded by eight Liverpool players who are unable to stop his goal-bound header in the 1998 FA Cup final.*

INTRODUCTION

The Premiership

The host of ingenious stadiums that grace the planet the world over have been crucial in the meteoric rise of that most popular sport – football. Today, the Premiership survives and continues to develop fast-paced with the likes of huge advertising deals, sponsorships and high-profile transfers, but it is the stadiums where titles are won and lost and where football clubs from the boardroom to the players and spectators alike can glean most satisfaction from what the sport has to offer.

When the Premiership first took shape during the 1992-93 season, after the breakaway from the Football League who had overseen the national leagues for more than a century, there were 22 clubs in the top flight. The founder members were: Arsenal, Aston Villa, Blackburn Rovers, Chelsea, Coventry City, Everton, Ipswich Town, Leeds United, Liverpool, Manchester City, Manchester United, Norwich City, Oldham Athletic, Queens Park Rangers, Sheffield United, Sheffield Wednesday, Southampton, Tottenham Hotspur and Wimbledon. It was an interesting campaign where Manchester United proved their worth as champions while Crystal Palace, Middlesbrough and Nottingham Forest suffered the disappointment of relegation.

The following season saw Newcastle United and West Ham United both climb their way up into the echelons of premier sides, while Swindon Town made their first ever appearance in the top flight. The campaign proved just as dramatic and it was no surprise that Manchester United retained their championship status or that Swindon Town's stint in the top flight was over when they were relegated to the First Division together with Oldham Athletic and Sheffield United.

The 1994-95 season still saw the Premiership hosting 22 clubs with Crystal Palace bouncing back to the top, along with Nottingham Forest, while Leicester City put in a first appearance. But this time, reigning champions Manchester United were knocked off the top spot by a concerted effort from Blackburn Rovers. Crystal Palace continued their "see-saw" approach and were relegated once more alongside Leicester City who had also managed just one season in the Premiership. Norwich City and Ipswich Town, however, joined Palace and Leicester back in Division One and – with the Premier League slimming down to 20 teams – Bolton and Middlesbrough grabbed the only two promotion places available.

Manchester United managed to reclaim their crown at the end of the 1995-96 season while Bolton Wanderers, after just one season in the Premiership, licked their wounds and resigned themselves to at least a season in Division One. The two other relegated teams were Manchester City and Queens Park Rangers, while Derby County, Sunderland and Leicester City were promoted to the top flight. Continuing their form, Alex Ferguson's side once again took the title in the 1996-97 campaign to make it four wins in five years while Sunderland, Middlesbrough and Nottingham Forest suffered the heartbreak of relegation. Barnsley fans, however, couldn't have been more overjoyed as the Yorkshire club secured its place in the top flight for the first time ever, along with Crystal Palace and Bolton (again).

Such is the ferocity in which the Premiership title is contested, Newcastle fans were ecstatic by the return of Kevin Keegan as manager in January 2008.

In what was becoming a regular occurrence , the newly-promoted sides all struggled during the 1997-98 campaign but unusually all three filled the relegation places come May. Arsenal were crowned champions before Manchester United once again claimed the title in 1998-99. The season was also to prove pivotal for Bradford City who found themselves in the top flight for the first time since 1922.

The 1999-2000 season saw reigning champions Manchester United once again claim the title while Wimbledon, Sheffield Wednesday and Watford all suffered relegation. Manchester City, Ipswich Town and Charlton Athletic were all promoted to the Premiership but the following campaign saw few changes. Manchester United claimed a hat-trick of Premiership crowns while their neighbors City were once again relegated to Division One (alongside Coventry City and Bradford City). Blackburn Rovers, Bolton Wanderers and Fulham earned the right to ply their trade with the best in the country.

However, during the 2001-02 season the Old Trafford outfit were knocked off the top spot, once again by Arsenal, but found their form and won back the title during the following campaign (2002-03). This was also the season that saw Portsmouth and Wolverhampton Wanderers make their debuts in the Premiership while Sunderland suffered bitter disappointment with just 19 points for their efforts all season, making them the first Premier League side to score less than 20 during a campaign.

The 2003-04 season saw Arsenal claim the championship from Manchester United for the third time since the Premiership began while Wolves, disappointingly, were relegated to Division One with Leicester City and Leeds United. The 2004-05 campaign saw Crystal Palace competing in the top flight once again – with Norwich City

An all too familiar sight for Derby County fans during 2007-08 as their team concede another goal. The Rams scored on average one goal to their opponents' four throughout the season.

and West Brom – but it was the resurgent Chelsea who claimed the Premier League title for the first time. Palace and Norwich found themselves sliding through the trapdoor after a 12-month stay along with Southampton.

Wigan Athletic, celebrating their first ever appearance in the top flight, West Ham United and Sunderland were the newcomers at the start of the 2005-06 campaign. Unlike Arsenal, who have managed one season at a time as champions, Chelsea went on to claim their second successive title. It was to prove a massive blow for Sunderland, however, who managed to amass a record low of just 15 points from their 38 games. Their relegation counterparts were Birmingham City and West Brom.

The new campaign, however, would see Reading enjoying their first time in top flight football. Also promoted alongside the Berkshire club were Sheffield United and Watford. The latter two teams both found life in the fast lane too hard to handle in 2006-07 and returned to the Football League Championship but the Royals finished in a very respectable eighth place. Having missed the top spot for three consecutive seasons, Manchester United were back in the driving seat and claimed their ninth championship title in 15 years.

Despite their previous disappointment, Sunderland were promoted from the Championship alongside Birmingham City and Derby County. The 2007-08 season saw a three-way race for the title between Arsenal, Chelsea and Manchester United but the dream was over by April for the Rams who found themselves earning the unwanted recognition of becoming the team to be relegated earliest in a Premiership season.

Several clubs have struggled following relegation from the Premiership and have gone on to suffer further relegations.

Barnsley, Leeds United, Nottingham Forest, Oldham Athletic, QPR and Sheffield Wednesday have all dropped to the third tier of English football. Bradford City, Swindon Town and MK Dons (formerly Wimbledon), however, have all ended up in the basement division. The good news for all those teams who do want to make it to the promised land, though, is that it can be done. During the inaugural Premiership season (1992-93) four clubs were languishing in the third level – Bolton won promotion to Division One, Reading and Fulham finished mid-table in the Second Division while Wigan were relegated to the new Division Three – but today are current Premiership clubs.

The evolution of football

There are two explanations as to how football may have been given its name. One widely held belief is that the word "football" is derived from the action of a foot kicking a ball, however, the other, and lesser known explanation is that football originated from a number of medieval games which were played on foot, as opposed to horseback. The oldest documented record of an activity related to football is found in China from around 476-221 BC where a game known as *cuju* or "kick ball" was played. This ancient game required the players to kick a leather ball through a hole in a piece of silk that was held fast between two 30-foot poles. Later, during the Han Dynasty (206 BC-220 AD) rules were established and variations of the game began to spread to Japan and Korea. By the Tang Dynasty, the traditional ball (stuffed with feathers) was replaced by a ball filled with air and kick ball was turned into a profession. The ancient Greeks and Romans also devised a variety of ball games which involved players using their feet, although many of these may have been forerunners of rugby rather than football. Pre-historic ball

games were also traditionally played by many indigenous peoples across the globe. Inuit people in Greenland were reported to have played a form of football as early as 1586 while Native Americans were recorded in the early 17th century playing *pahsaheman*. In Australia, *marn grook* was played by aborigines (a ball game very similar to football) but the general consensus is that football as we recognize it today has its origins in Western Europe and particularly the UK.

The game that originated most notably in England, may have coincided with the arrival of the Romans, but there is not enough evidence to substantiate that there was a link between the two. However, the medieval period saw a rise in the popularity of Shrovetide football. It is possible, that the game of football that the English became hooked on, in fact, arrived from across the English Channel from Brittany and Normandy in France where a game known as *La Soule* or *Choule*, was extremely popular. This game could have arrived in England after the Norman Conquest. Often referred to as "mob football" – due to the unlimited number of players involved – the game was played between neighboring towns and villages using, for example, an inflated pig's bladder as a ball. In a similar fashion to the origins of other sports, such as steeplechasing, it was usual to try and be the first team to reach a decided landmark, particularly church towers. Such was the popularity of these annual Shrovetide matches with people heaving and shoving each other en-masse in pursuit of a small object that a number of English towns still adopt the pastime today.

The first properly documented description of football was written between 1174 and 1183 by William FitzStephen in London when he observed some youths playing the game during Shrove Tuesday festivities. However, FitzStephen's account does not

The game saw a huge increase in popularity during the wars. Here, fans flock to St James' Park in March 1930.

The Second World War wreaked havoc on many grounds. Here, a bomb damaged pitch is repaired.

actually mention that anyone kicked the ball, although he does go into great detail about the enthusiasm of the spectators who were clearly caught up in the drama of the action on the field. Then, in 1314, the Mayor of London, Nicholas de Farndone, banned football which was being enjoyed by the English aristocracy. Although the decree is written in French – a common language amongst the aristocracy at the time – there is a clear reference to a "foot ball" and it is thought to be the earliest reference to the sport. However, the earliest mention of a ball being kicked came seven years later in 1321 during a game in Shouldham, Norfolk. More than 40 years later and football was banned across England by King Edward III as an "idle game" and King Henry IV forbade the levying of money in "foteball" in 1409. By the end of the 15th century, football was beginning to take shape as we know it. The first description of a "kicking game" came from documented evidence of a match in Nottinghamshire where players used their feet to propel the ball from one end of the field to the other and as well as kicking, rolled the ball across the ground (also using their feet) where opposing teams kicked and "dribbled" the ball in opposite directions. The game developed and became widespread fairly quickly. In 1526, Henry VIII ordered a pair of football boots to be made especially for him and by 1580, there were reports that women were beginning to form their own teams. Goals first came to prominence during the late 16th century when they were used in Cornish hurling. "Goles" were also scored in camp-ball, a violent form of football which was particularly popular in East Anglia.

Despite the popularity of the developing game, football faced its fair amount of criticism and disapproval. Often games were rowdy and many attempts were made to ban them. Between 1324 and 1667 there were more than 30 royal and local bans. However, like golf, which was also banned at a national and local level, the popularity of the game meant that it wouldn't be held back for long. Some bans were seen as a necessary means to an end. Edward III, for example, banned the sport in London because it took people away from practising archery (which was necessary for war) just as golf had done.

While the ancient and very early ball games were associated with peasants, the rules and the establishment of modern codes seem to have originated in the English public (private) school system. The first change came when football was transformed from its "mob" culture, where as many people as possible joined in, to a highly organised team sport. Many former students of English public schools began writing about the football they played which indicates that it was here that boundaries, rules and details were established. Football games were codified by the schools so that each could present a team to play other learning establishments and this was also when games which involved "kicking", "carrying" or "running" began to take a more modern shape. Although there are many descriptions and accounts given of the games played during the 16th century, the most detailed description comes from the *Book of Games* (1660) by Francis Willughby who expertly describes each team scoring goals on a marked out field. The book also contains a diagram of a football field and goes on to mention tactics (as in a player is selected to "guard" the goal). The offside rule was created in the late 18th century (in English schoolboy football) , if a player simply stood between the ball and the goal. The rule stated that the player was not allowed to pass the ball forward, but this was later developed, and many schools established their own offside rules.

Those who were more privileged than the majority were able to indulge in sports and football was quickly established within the public schooling system as a way of encouraging competitiveness while keeping pupils fit. However, for those not quite so fortunate, football was a pastime for the few. With six working days each week consisting of twelve or more hours a day, there was no time for football. In addition, many children were part of the backbone of the UK's work force and were toiling alongside their parents. There was little, if any, time or energy for the sport that would one day grip the nation.

The Cambridge rules were established in 1848 at Cambridge University which clearly showed that the "kicking" game was preferred although no record of this document now exists (a revised version is still in existence). Leather covers were introduced to the early pig's bladders to allow the ball to keep its shape, and in 1851, shoemakers Richard Lindon and William Gilbert, from Rugby, exhibited round and oval balls at the Great Exhibition in London. Just four years later and Charles Goodyear, the American inventor, had created a spherical football with vulcanized rubber panels which he exhibited in Paris. By the late 1850s, many football clubs had been formed (following various codes) and the Sheffield Football Club – founded in 1857 – had its own code of football, although it would later become recognized as the world's oldest club which played association football.

The Football Association (FA)

The modern day game of football has its roots firmly in the foundations of the Football Association (FA) which was established in 1863 in England. By this time, several clubs had already formed and were beginning to establish themselves as the forerunners of the modern day sport, but a universal code was required so that

Crowds as great as this are certainly a thing of the past in today's Premiership. It is also unlikely you will see a policeman chasing a goose across the pitch.

clubs could play each other fairly without prejudice or confusion. Up until the formation of the FA, rules had to be decided between clubs on the day of the match so that they could play one another. Several clubs met in London to establish the universal code and, although its effect wasn't immediate, it begin to turn what was an amateur game (played historically by school boys) into a professional sport. Players began to start playing for money while businessmen and other entrepreneurs began to take advantage of the huge amounts that could be made by charging spectators to come and watch their star players perform. The speed at which football then took off – around the globe – was nothing short of phenomenal once professional status was given to the sport. The Cambridge rules were adapted a number of times before Ebenezer Cobb Morley (1831-1924) proposed a governing body should be set up. Morley was the FA's first secretary between 1863 and 1866 and is often described as the "Father of Football". He drafted the first rules of the game which are still played the world over today. The first FA rules have elements that are no longer applicable in Association Football, however, they are still evident in Rugby Union and Australian rules football. As well as rules for conduct, the laws also stipulated a maximum length and breadth of the football pitch, the kicking off procedure and a definition of terms. Having established the sport in professional terms, it was time to start looking at competitions.

Sheffield and Notts County (formerly Nottingham) immediately began a long tradition of playing an annual fixture by FA rules. Chesterfield and Stoke then joined the code and it was now established that each team should have eleven players. Round balls were now a pre-requisite and a Sheffield versus London game in 1866 gave the FA the opportunity to see how the code was affecting the game. It was then that handling the ball was abolished (apart from the goalkeeper) and a national competition was proposed.

The first FA Cup took place in 1872 and the final saw 2,000 paying spectators turn up to watch Wanderers against Royal Engineers. Wanderers claimed the first FA Cup in a 1-0 victory and the huge success of the competition saw the advent of many more clubs applying to take part. The FA code had to be accepted by any football club wishing to take part and this quickly established a universal set of rules for players and clubs to abide by. The first "cup" was purchased (at a cost of £20.00) and fifteen clubs took part in the competition. By the following year, a league competition was proposed with twelve football clubs (who would later become the Football League's founding members). FA secretary Charles Alcock was instrumental in championing the first ever international match. He advertised in Glasgow newspapers announcing an international between England and Scotland. As a result, a Scottish team was quickly established which saw the Scots draw 0-0 against their rivals. Professional football was legalized by the FA in 1885 but there was a national wage limit. The last amateur team to win the FA Cup was the Old Etonians who beat northern club, Blackburn Rovers, in 1882.

The earliest clubs

It is possible that an organization of football players existed in London between 1421 and 1423, where the players were listed as a "fraternity" when they played in the hall of the Brewers' Company in London. However, many very early clubs did not use the word football in their name. One of the first documented football clubs is the Foot Ball Club of John Hope in Edinburgh, Scotland, between 1824 and 1841, and a club in Newcastle in 1848 was a club that played "cricket, quoits and football". Barnes Club (in London) was formed in 1839 while Guy's Hospital Football Club was founded in 1843. Dublin University Football Club was established at Trinity College in 1854 and has a well-documented, continuous history, although today, the college is renowned for its rugby union. Cambridge University played to Cambridge rules from 1848 onwards on the club ground known as Parkers Piece where football had been a favourite since 1838. While, as already mentioned, Sheffield Football Club (founded in 1857) was the oldest non-university or school club.

The history of the stadium

Today's modern stadiums do a great deal more than host prolific football matches. Many stadia are used as venues for a variety of events including concerts, conferences and a host of other sporting activities. Originating from the Greek word "stadion" meaning "a stand" for spectators to stand, sit and watch an event, the oldest stadium is in Olympia, Greece, where the Olympic Games were held from 776 BC onwards. But, despite the Greeks claiming a first, the Romans were quick to catch on and the oldest, most infamous stadiums in Rome are the Colosseum and the Stadium of Domitian. Although most commonly used with the sport of football, stadiums – designed to house outdoor sports, rather than indoor sports (arenas) – are also associated with American football, baseball, Gaelic football, hurling, rugby and other games that require a large pitch.

Since the 1990s, for safety reasons, it has been a requirement by law that all stadiums in the UK are all-seater. However, in the US, many stadiums have areas for spectators to stand and all-seater stadiums are not particularly common. Designing, building and

A computer generated impression of Liverpool's proposed 60,000 seater stadium announced in July 2007.

constructing a stadium is an expensive business. The facilities that are required, the regulations that have to be adhered to, all incur huge costs which have to be met. In order to help football clubs achieve their aims and the stadium of their dreams, it has become commonplace to offer sponsorship of various stands within a specific stadium. The trend began in the 1970s, but grew rapidly throughout the 1990s.

There seems to have been a pattern of development that is common to almost all the major English football stadiums. Many were originally constructed in the late 1800s and were first developed and modernized during the 1920s and 1930s. There was a flurry of activity across the board when stadium lights were introduced in the mid to late 1950s allowing clubs to play into the evening. Another decade of change came about during the 1970s when there was a revolutionary push to develop stadia, however, the biggest changes came about during the early 1990s following the tragic events at Hillsborough in April 1989. The face of the football stadium was about to change – for the better – forever with the advent of the Taylor Report and the huge crowds that had been commonplace throughout the course of the sport's history were about to be limited in all-seater stadiums.

Many victories are won and lost at stadiums across the globe. These events can bring about huge changes for players, clubs and fans alike, however, for some stadiums, the catastrophic events that occur within them and those that cause loss of life, mean that they are firmly etched on the memories of all. Hillsborough, Valley Parade, Burnden Park and the Heysel Stadium are probably more widely known for the horrific events that took place within their parameters rather than for any sporting event.

Hillsborough saw 96 Liverpool fans lose their lives when they

An ambulance on the Hillsborough pitch, about to rush the injured to hospital in April 1989.

The stand burns while fans look on at Valley Parade, Bradford in 1985.

were crushed to death when too many fans tried to enter the stadium having endured a bottle-neck through the turnstiles at the Leppings Lane End of the stadium. The impact of 5,000 or so fans trying to get through gates opened by the police in order to avoid a crush was not properly monitored and those fans at the front of the terrace were crushed against the high fencing (deemed necessary to combat hooligans) by the sheer weight of the crowd behind them. The match had already started by the time the time the problem was noticed and the referee brought the match to an end after just six minutes of play. Today, there are memorials at both Anfield (near the Shankly Gates), home of Liverpool, and the Hillsborough stadium itself.

One of the contributing factors at Hillsborough was the high fencing that was erected to stop any away fans, visiting Sheffield Wednesday's stadium, from causing any problems to players and opposing fans. Sadly, football hooligans had long been a tradition with English football and the fencing was seen as a necessary element to any stadium.

The event at one stadium, Heysel, in Brussels was to prove the catalyst for such fencing. Throughout the 1970s and 1980s, large gangs of football fans intent on causing trouble had built up a reputation for extreme behaviour. This was particularly highlighted at Heysel in May 1985 when, during a match between Liverpool and Juventus (Italy), 39 people lost their lives. One hour before kick-off, a fence separating Liverpool and Juventus fans was breached by the English supporters. Having nowhere to go, the Juventus fans began retreating putting enormous pressure on a dilapidated wall. The wall collapsed. However, despite the deaths of mainly Italian fans, the match went ahead as scheduled to try to avert further confrontation. English football clubs were banned from all European competitions by UEFA (which was lifted after five years) and Liverpool were further excluded for an additional three years. This ban had a major impact on English football on and off the pitch. Clubs began imposing much stricter rules on fans to try and limit the trouble-makers, however, it wasn't until the Hillsborough disaster that the main reforms took place. But, not every disaster can be attributed to hooligans and insufficient policing.

On 11 May 1985 a vicious fire quickly took hold of one side of the Valley Parade football stadium in Bradford during a match between Bradford City and Lincoln City. The fire is thought to have started when a spectator failed to extinguish a cigarette and it fell down beneath the wooden seating and onto a pile of rubbish which had accumulated over more than 20 years. Although fire equipment reached the white smoke rising out of the seating quickly, within 90 seconds it was clear to all concerned that the fire was dangerously out of control. In just two minutes of being spotted, the flash fire had engulfed the main stand. Many of those towards the back of the stand were overcome by toxic smoke and 56 people lost their lives. Countless acts of heroism by supporters and police prevented the death toll from being even higher and fans who had escaped onto the pitch managed to help save a great number of other supporters. The inquiry into the disaster led to new legislation to improve safety and the construction of new wooden grandstands were banned. There are two memorials at Valley Parade which was re-developed including a sculpture and a black marble fascia on which the names of those who died are inscribed.

The first major English stadium disaster came at Burnden Park in 1946. With football enjoying a boom following the end of the Second World War, spectators were eager to attend the FA Cup tie between Bolton Wanderers and Stoke City and an estimated crowd

Women and children are passed over the heads of the crowd during the crush in which 33 football fans died during the March 1946 FA Cup tie between Bolton and Stoke at Burnden Park.

RIGHT: Artificial lighting rigs in use on the pitch at the Reebok Stadium. The technology enables grass growth during the whole winter season providing natural grass of extremely good quality.

of 85,000 people flocked to Burnden Park. However, the sheer numbers in the crowd caused mass congestion which led to 33 people being crushed to death against the barriers in the Embankment end. It would become the greatest tragedy in British football until the Ibrox Park disaster in 1971 (Ibrox had already seen its fair share of tragedy when a section of stand collapsed in 1902 during a Scotland-England international).

Despite the difficulties and the tragic events that have taken place, many more matches have passed without incident in some of the most prestigious stadiums in English football. Many of those are steeped in history – Villa Park, Craven Cottage, Elland Road, Old Trafford and Stamford Bridge, to name but a few – while others have been designed to bring the club and its surroundings into the 21st century, such as the Emirates Stadium, Reebok Stadium, Ricoh Arena, Pride Park, Walkers Stadium and the City of Manchester Stadium. From the first stadiums, with supporters balancing on rubble left over from preparing the pitch for action, to the latest high-tech innovations with lights utilized over the pitch to stimulate grass-growth to undersoil heating systems to prevent pitches from freezing over, this book is bound to capture the imagination.

ARSENAL

Address:	Emirates Stadium, Drayton Park, London N5 1BU
Website:	www.arsenal.com
Ground capacity:	60,432
Pitch dimensions:	105m x 68m
Opened:	2006
Premiership member:	1992-
Record attendance:	60,161 v Manchester United, 3 November 2007, Premier League

With a new millennium on the horizon, the 1990s saw Arsenal wanting to develop a larger stadium more in line with that of other large European football clubs. Although a host of locations were considered, it was preferable for the club's ground to remain close to the original site at Highbury. With sponsorship from Emirates Airline of £100 million, it was publicized in October 2004 that the new stadium, which lies 500 metres from the old site on previously industrial railway land, would be known as the Emirates Stadium for the next 15 years. Some, however, continue to call the stadium by its original name of Ashburton Grove, after the site on which it was built.

Emirates Stadium, in Holloway, north London opened in July 2006, after a three-year delay, designed by architects HOK Sport. The company worked with AYH construction consultants and Buro Happold engineers to create a four-tiered bowl with roofing confined to the stands that were constructed by Sir Robert Alpine. It made the stadium the second largest Premiership ground after Old Trafford. It is the third largest stadium in London – only Twickenham and Wembley are larger. A significant design element is the open space contoured through the upper tier with a canted inward roof which allows as much light and airflow onto the pitch as possible. Highbury House (in homage to the old stadium) is where the official offices of the club are housed in the north east of the ground where the bust of Herbert Chapman is now located.

With season tickets costing up to almost £2,000, the ground holds a capacity crowd of more than 60,000. Arsenal hosts its away supporters in the lower tier behind the south goal and has a seating capacity of up to 4,500, while a further 4,500 seats can be provided in the upper tier. Providing supporters with a capacity of 9,000 complies with the 15% requirement for domestic cup competitions.

The pitch itself is 105 metres by 68 metres and is the joint-largest of all the Premiership pitches with a grassed area of 113 metres by 76 metres. Running north to south, just as the ground did at Highbury, the dugouts and players' tunnel is situated on the west side of the ground. Arsenal is renowned for its exceptional playing surface and this was a major consideration in the design of the new stadium. Two giant screens are suspended from the roof in the north west and south east corners of the stadium and a third screen has been mooted.

Two railway bridges connect the stadium to Drayton Park and are named after the Clock End and North Bank bridges in honour of the stands at Highbury in the Arsenal stadium which gave the club its home between September 1913 and May 2006. Fondly referred to as Highbury, Arsenal Stadium was redeveloped twice during its long history in the 1930s and late 1980s early 1990s. In 1913, Woolwich Arsenal moved to Highbury where they leased the recreation fields of St John's College of Divinity. The stadium was designed by Archibald Leitch and consisted of a single stand on the eastern side with banked terraces on the remaining sides. The stadium had a capacity crowd of 73,000 during its heyday, but upon closure had a reduced number of 38,419. Today, the site is being redeveloped, however, parts of the east and west stands will be incorporated into the plans.

Arsenal's name is proudly emblazoned outside the Emirates Stadium.

OPPOSITE: An aerial view of the Emirates Stadium in April 2007.

LEFT: Action during the UEFA Champions League match between Arsenal and PSV Eindhoven on 7 March 2007.

ABOVE: The Gunners' pair of cannons on guard outside the Armoury at the Emirates Stadium.

RIGHT: The first match at the Emirates was Dennis Bergkamp's testimonial against Ajax in July 2006.

OPPOSITE: An aerial view of Highbury, Arsenal's home from 1913-2006.

LEFT: Arsenal host Wigan Athletic on 7 May 2006 in the last match to be played at Highbury.

ASTON VILLA

Address:	Villa Park, Birmingham B6 6HE
Website:	www.avfc.co.uk
Ground capacity:	42,551
Pitch dimensions:	105m x 68m
Opened:	1897
Premiership member:	1992-
Record attendance:	76,588 v Derby County, 2 March 1946, FA Cup

Villa Park, began life as the Aston Lower Grounds in 1897, at a cost of £16,400. Today, it is a UEFA four-star stadium, located on Trinity Road in the Aston area of Birmingham, hence the name. It is home to Aston Villa with a maximum all-seated capacity of 42, 551 although there are plans to extend the seating to accommodate up to 50,000 spectators.

Aston Villa have been associated with Villa Park since its inauguration in 1897 – the first match here was between Aston Villa and Blackburn Rovers on 17 April that same year – but the first international on the pitch took place in 1899. In fact, Villa Park was the first Premiership ground to host international football in three different centuries, the 1800s, 1900s and the 2000s. The ground can also boast having held the most FA Cup semi-finals in the history of the sport; 55 semi-finals have been played here in total.

Built in the grounds of a former stately home, the site was originally designated land for an amusement park during the Victorian era. When Aston Hall became home to Sir Thomas Holte, the site was used for his own personal kitchen garden and fishpond. Sir Thomas' name was then taken for the original first stand – the Holte End. The first spectators at Villa Park would have been mainly standing with a total capacity of 40,000. A cycle track, made of concrete, surrounded the original pitch alongside a running track.

The site was bought by Aston Villa in 1911 at a total cost of £11,750 and, under supervision from director Frederick Rinder, the first plans were drawn up. The initial ambitious ideas were abandoned, however, at the outbreak of the First World War. The Trinity Road Stand was completed eleven years later in 1922 and consisted of impressive stained glass windows, a sweeping staircase and mosaics, all created by renowned architect Archie Leitch.

Today, the Holte End stand consists of two tiers and is one of the largest stands behind the goal of any European football stadium. The North Stand and is now considered "dated" having been constructed in the 1970s. The Doug Ellis Stand, (which seats the away fans and is named after the club's former chairman) sits opposite the Trinity Road Stand, renowned for its modern look with its three tier seating and row of executive boxes. Originally, the Doug Ellis Stand was called the Witton Lane Stand – a name that is still used by some of the club's current fans. Floodlights were added in 1958 to the ground.

Despite being home to Aston Villa for more than a century, Villa Park has also had its other uses. It played host to numerous athletic and cycling events prior to the First World War. It has been chosen as one of only six stadiums which will be used during the summer Olympics in 2012 which will entitle the ground to funding for use in expanding the stadium.

RIGHT: The exterior of the Trinity Road Stand.

RIGHT: Villa Park from the air.

OPPOSITE: Aston Villa entertain Manchester United during the 2007-08 season.

Aston Villa host Spurs in a Premiership match in January 2003.

The gates outside Villa Park.

BARNSLEY

Address:	Oakwell Stadium, Grove Street, Barnsley S71 1ET
Website:	www.barnsleyfc.co.uk
Ground capacity:	23,186
Pitch dimensions:	91m x 61m
Opened:	1887
Premiership member:	1997-98
Record attendance:	40,255 v Stoke City, 13 1936, FA Cup

Today, the Oakwell sports development is owned by Barnsley council, in South Yorkshire, and consists of a number of sites including an indoor training pitch, the main sports stadium, a smaller stadium and several other training pitches. The main site is the home of Barnsley FC and is operated by the Club. The name "Oakwell" generally refers to the main site, although the smaller parts of the stadium are officially included under the one name. Situated on Grove Street in Barnsley itself, the ground was inaugurated in 1887 where the Tykes – the nickname comes from the traditional belief that a Yorkshireman is rugged, hardworking and has immense pride – were founded and played their first game here in the Sheffield and District League under the supervision of their first manager Arthur Fairclough. The current capacity for the stadium is just over 23,000 although the ground's record attendance came in 1936 when more than 40,250 spectators turned out to watch Barnsley versus Stoke City.

The West Stand is the only part of the stadium that is original. Made up of two tiers, the seating dates from the early 1900s and is still a firm favourite with the fans. The upper tier is covered while the lower tier, from where spectators have a good vantage of the on-pitch action, is not. The roof of this stand is made of corrugated iron and is supported by a number of columns, and it is here that the main television gantry can be found. When match attendances were particularly high during the 1990s Barnsley were intent on developing the stand. All dreams were dashed in 2003, however, when the decline of the club's fortunes and their fall into administration saw the stadium and surrounding land purchased by Barnsley council. Although the development was abandoned, it did allow the club to remain in the League and creditors received their financial settlements. The seating capacity for the West Stand is 4,752.

The Enterprise PLC Stand was originally named the Pontefract Road End (also known as Ponty End) and was completed in the mid-1990s. However, the stand has also been known by other names including the Van Damme Stand and the ORA Stand (because of its former sponsors). With its current capacity of 4,508, the stand is also the site of the Club's box office, administration block, players' gym and shop. It was built with future development in mind and a second tier would be possible without making huge structural changes to the existing construction. The East Stand was completed two years earlier than the Enterprise Stand in 1993 and comprises two tiers with a capacity of 7,492. The original building on this spot consisted of a large covered terrace but, funded partly by the Football Trust, the new stand incorporated the first executive boxes at a football club in Yorkshire.

The East Stand, Corner Stand and North Stand were all designed by NYP Architects and the latter is the most recent of the stadium's seating areas. With capacity for 5,000 spectators, the North Stand is a large covered single tier. The Corner Stand was built around the same time as the Enterprise and East Stands and was completed in 1998. It is an unusual three level construction which consists of additional executive facilities and was originally known as "The Welcome Windows" Stand, named after its enclosed design. Here 202 spectators can gain access to the East Stand.

ABOVE: Barnsley play Manchester United in 1964. As can be seen from the crowd, the ground's capacity was much larger in those days.

RIGHT: Oakwell from the air – the West Stand is the only original structure still standing, although plans have been announced for its replacement.

BIRMINGHAM CITY

Address:	St Andrews Stadium Birmingham B9 4NH
Website:	www.bcfc.com
Ground capacity:	30,079
Pitch dimensions:	92m x 62m
Opened:	1906
Premiership member:	2002-06, 2007-
Record attendance:	66,844 v Everton, 11 1939, FA Cup

St Andrews stadium is home to Birmingham City and first opened in 1906, however, football matches had been played in the area since 1875. Using a piece of wasteland just off Arthur Street in the city, Small Health Alliance played their first ever match against a team from Aston in another part of the city, Holte Wanderers (later to become Aston Villa). The team's first enclosed ground was incorporated the following year for the 1876-77 season and a crowd of around 500 spectators gathered for the inaugural match in September 1876 at the 3,000 capacity ground.

The team then moved to Muntz Street before taking up their permanent residence at St Andrews in 1906. The stadium had been completed a year earlier when rent at Muntz Street had been increased from £5.00 to £300.00 annually. Deciding that the former ground was unsatisfactory (it was never particularly popular with the home team or visiting sides) St Andrews was found by Harry Morris. Situated just off Garrison Lane and Bordesley Green, Morris was convinced that his "find" was the perfect spot for a grand football arena. Harry Pumfrey was the local man approached to draw up plans for the new ground. As a Blue's fan, Pumfrey took his role seriously.

Although not an architect (Pumfrey was in fact a carpenter), he and T W Turley worked tirelessly to complete the ground for which they refused to accept payment.

The largest crowed that ever flocked to St Andrews was in 1939 when 67,341 spectators turned out for a match against Everton on 11 in the FA Cup fifth round. Capacity has been continually reduced at the stadium since before the Second World War. It started at 68,000 but was down to just over 53,000 by the mid-1960s. By the end of the 1980s, capacity had further dropped to around 38,000 and today, the stadium has capacity of just over 30,000.

The pitch itself is 92 metres long and 62 metres wide and covers former wasteland which had to be drained of two large pools of water. These were then filled in with rubble and local residents were asked to dump their rubbish to one side of the pitch so that a large grassed embankment could be created, known as the Spion Kop. Terracing was then created from disused railway sleepers and work began on the Grandstand, which ran along Garrison Lane. The newly finished stadium was open by Sir John Holder in front of 32,000 fans who braved the appalling weather to watch City in Division One on 26 December 1906.

Development at St Andrews since the mid-20th century had been minimal, but following the Taylor Report in the aftermath of the Hillsborough tragedy whereby all stadiums had to become fully seated, plans were drawn up and renovation to the ground began in 1994. It was officially opened by Baroness Trumpington in November that same year and further development was planned at the Railway Stand. The new stand, which also incorporates the players' dressing rooms, was then opened in 1999.

Birmingham City finally won promotion to the Premiership in May 2002 and have since cemented their position as a top-flight side, although they did suffer relegation in 2006 but bounced back at the first attempt.

Birmingham play Arsenal in January 2003.

ABOVE: *The sun sets on City's match against Manchester United in September 2007.*

RIGHT: *An aerial shot of St Andrews, home to Birmingham City for more than 100 years.*

BLACKBURN ROVERS

Address:	Ewood Park, Blackburn BB2 4JF
Website:	www.rovers.co.uk
Ground capacity:	31,154
Pitch dimensions:	105m x 66m
Opened:	1890
Premiership member:	1992-99, 2001-
Record attendance:	62,522 v Bolton Wanderers, 2 March 1929, FA Cup

As the only football club to have won the FA Cup three times in consecutive seasons, Blackburn Rovers are entitled to display the club's crest on the corner flags of Ewood Park, their home ground since 1890. Ewood Park had opened officially some eight years earlier as a multi-function sports stadium and now consists of the Darwen End, the Riverside Stand (based alongside the River Darwen), Blackburn End and the Jack Walker Stand, named after the local industrialist and Blackburn Rovers supporter.

Like many other Premiership grounds, the stadium saw little development during the 1900s, but was brought into the 21st century by new regulatory changes, facility requirements, enforced renovations and a need to generally bring the site up to scratch. A fire in part of the Nuttall Street Stand saw the structure replaced with a stand complete with executive boxes in the early 1980s, and following the declaration that the old Riverside Stand was unsafe, this was also rebuilt. Jack Walker steel was brought in for the rebuild and it was renamed the Fraser Eagle Stand for the 2007-08 season following sponsorship. (This is the only section of Ewood Park that pre-dates the 21st century.)

Jack Walker bought Blackburn Rovers in 1991 and redevelopment of the stadium took off in earnest. The Darwen End, Blackburn End and Nuttall Street Stand were all demolished and reconstruction resulted in the latter being renamed the Jack Walker Stand in honour of the club's owner with seating for 11,000. Both the Darwen End and the Blackburn End are mirror images of each other seating 8,000 spectators respectively. The Darwen End is also completely allocated to away fans.

The players' dressing rooms, media and television facilities are all housed in the Jack Walker stand, while the boardroom (which was originally located in the Nuttall Street Stand) is now to be found at the Blackburn End. The pitch itself is 105 metres long and 66 metres wide while the stadium is the oldest of any ground in the Premier League. It is also the fourteenth largest stadium of any Premiership club, however, it has the lowest average attendance in terms of its percentage of capacity.

With Rovers fans having been starved off success for so long, the pairing of Alan Shearer and Chris Sutton brought the Premiership title to Ewood Park in 1994-95 (after the club had finished runners-up the previous season) but fortunes declined and Rovers were relegated in 1999. Their stay in the Football League lasted just two seasons and, under Mark Hughes, they have proved to be a difficult side to beat.

Since 2003, attendance figures have been declining steadily and today, around 25 percent of seats remain unsold on match days. In just over four years, more than 5,000 previously committed fans have failed to buy tickets to watch Rovers (despite qualifying for the UEFA Cup), and as a result, the club reduced prices to try and encourage former supporters back into the stands. However, in terms of the size of the city (and population of Blackburn) Ewood Park has a high ratio of fans and the number of seats filled on match days represent around one fifth of the city's total population. Capacity at the ground is 31,154 while the average attendance during 2006-07 was just over 21,200. Not bad for a city with around 105,000 inhabitants.

LEFT AND ABOVE: Two views of Ewood Park from different perspectives in May 2005.

Matt Derbyshire equalises against Middlesbrough in January 2008.

Ewood Park, pictured in July 1997.

LEFT: Blackburn play Everton under a spectacular sky in August 2006.

ABOVE: Politicians also find use for football grounds. Here Foreign Secretary Jack Straw meets US Secretary of State Condoleezza Rice in March 2006.

BOLTON WANDERERS

Address:	Reebok Stadium, Burnden Way, Lostock, Bolton BL6 6JW
Website:	www.bwfc.co.uk
Ground capacity:	28,500
Pitch dimensions:	105m x 68m
Opened:	1997
Premiership member:	1995-96, 1997-98, 2001-
Record attendance:	69,912 v Manchester City, 18 1933, FA Cup

Life began for Bolton Wanderers in the Burnden area of Bolton situated approximately one mile from the city centre. The ground was opened in 1895 and was to remain the club's home for 102 years. It was finally closed in 1997 when the Bolton Wanderers moved to their current site in Horwich and the Reebok Stadium, more commonly referred to as "The Reebok".

Today, the old site of Burnden Park has been redeveloped and now houses a huge superstore. But, it was very different more than 100 years before, when the ground could accommodate around 60,000 supporters. However, the Burnden Park was also instrumental in changing the laws with regard to capacity crowds. In March 1946, with an over capacity crowd of 85,000 or so people, thirty three fans died of asphyxiation due to congestion. It was the worst disaster in English football's history at the time and led to the Moelwyn Hughes Report which strongly recommended limits on the size of attendances allowed at football grounds. During the final 20 years of Burnden Park's existence total numbers of spectators were dramatically reduced in line with the report and new legislation made sure that each and every club had a capacity limit.

The Reebok was purpose-built as a state of the art football stadium in 1997 and opened that same year. But the move proved unpopular with many of the club's fans who wanted to stay at Burnden Park. Despite the modern facilities and larger capacity (the Reebok has a total capacity of 28,500) the fact that the stadium was built outside Bolton ensured the fans' commitment to the old ground so, in recognition of the former site, the road on which the new stadium was built was named Burnden Way.

The Premiership ground has four stands named The Debt Matters Stand, at the north end, the Woodford Group Stand to the south, while the east stand is named after Nat Lofthouse and is opposite the aptly named West Stand. The stadium is, unsurprisingly, named after its sponsor, Reebok.

In similar fashion to many other Premiership stadiums, football is not the only activity to take place at the Reebok. There is a hotel with function rooms (for business, weddings etc) and it is also used as an arena for big rock and pop acts; Oasis, Coldplay and Sir Elton John have all performed here). Other sporting events, including international rugby and boxing matches have also been hosted at the Reebok.

Back to the Premier League, and the first player to score at the stadium was Alan Thompson in a 1-1 draw against Spurs in September 1997. Three days later, the ground hosted its first League Cup match between Bolton and Leyton Orient. The first competitive match at the Reebok was won by Aston Villa in a 1-0 victory while the first FA Cup match took place on 1 January in 1999. Sadly, during the 2006-07 season, Bolton Wanderers suffered their first League crowd of less than 20,000 in October 2007 and since that time have only enjoyed more than 20,000 spectators at the Reebok on two occasions.

Bolton Wanderers have spent three spells in the Premiership with the current one being the most successful. They spent single seasons in the top flight in both 1995-96 and 1997-98 but qualified for the UEFA Cup in 2005-06.

LEFT: The Reebok Stadium has now been home to Bolton Wanderers for more than a decade.

The Trotters entertain Portsmouth in September 2005. The previous season had seen Bolton record their best ever Premiership finish of sixth.

Action from September 1947 as Bolton play host to Liverpool at Burnden Park. The ground's capacity at this time was more than 60,000.

BRADFORD CITY

Address:	Coral Windows Stadium, Valley Parade, Bradford, West Yorkshire BD8 7DY
Website:	www.bradfordcityfc.co.uk
Ground capacity:	25,136
Pitch dimensions:	103m x 64m
Opened:	1903
Premiership member:	1999-2001
Record attendance:	39,146 v Burnley, 11 March 1911, FA Cup

Known as the Coral Windows Stadium through sponsorship, Valley Parade, as it is also known, is home to Bradford City and was built in 1903. The ground was also opened that same year and today has a capacity of 25,136. Situated on the side of a valley (as the original name suggests), Valley Parade is cut into the valley to the west while the east side is raised above the sloping surface in the Manningham area of Bradford.

The stadium itself is divided into five stands consisting of the Carlsberg Stand, Sunwin Stand, Pulse Family Stand, East Stand and the TL Dallas Stand some of which are currently named after individual sponsors. The Carlsberg Stand, named after the sponsor, Carlsberg as it would suggest, was originally known as the Kop End while the Sunwin Stand is also known as the Main Stand. The TL Dallas Stand is traditionally known as the Bradford End (as it is the closest to the city centre) and was originally the stand designated for Bradford supporters. The Pulse Family Stand is also known as the North West Corner and the East Stand was originally named the Midland Road Stand. Today, away fans are accommodated in the TL Dallas Stand, but are also given a section of the East Stand if their numbers require it.

Each year, the Coral Windows Stadium holds a remembrance ceremony following the death of 56 spectators in a fire on 11 May 1985. It is thought that a carelessly discarded cigarette dropped down between the 85 year old wooden seating where it ignited litter in the Sunwin Stand. At the time, 11,000 fans were watching the final game of the season while celebrating Bradford's recent victory in the Third Division championship. The fire spread quickly engulfing the stand and wide-spread panic ensued. Ironically, the following day the wooden roof was to have been removed and replaced as it had already been deemed as unsafe. Small children and the former chairman of the club lost their lives alongside other fans that day and the tragedy was to see the start of improved safety conditions for spectators at many different sporting events and was escalated four years later with the advent of Hillsborough. Valley Parade was rebuilt and opened in December 1986.

The attendances at the ground have been fairly consistent throughout its history and the modern-day stadium saw a record crowd of 22,057 spectators for the Premiership match against Liverpool in May 2001. However, the highest attendance (which came before more stringent safety regulations were in place) came on 11 March 1911, when 39,146 fans turned up to watch the home team play Burnley in the fourth round of the FA Cup. The club went on to beat Newcastle's Toon Army in the final staged at Old Trafford that same year.

As well as playing host to Bradford City's matches, the Coral Windows Stadium, for a short time (during 2001 and 2002), was also home to the Bradford Bulls, the city's most prolific Rugby League Club. While here the Bulls won the 2001 Super League Title and the 2002 World Cup Challenge Title.

RIGHT: Although the club have been at Valley Parade since 1903, the stadium has been known by various sponsors' names in recent years.

RIGHT: An aerial view of Bradford City's Stadium.

OPPOSITE: The burnt out remains of the Bantams' Main South Parade Stand following the fire on 11 May 1985 that claimed 56 lives.

CHARLTON ATHLETIC

Address:	The Valley, Floyd Road, Charlton, London SE7 8BL
Website:	www.cafc.co.uk
Ground capacity:	27,113
Pitch dimensions:	105m x 66m
Opened:	1919
Premiership member:	1998-99, 2000-07
Record attendance:	75,031 v Aston Villa, 12 February 1938, FA Cup

After a particularly nomadic existence, the group of former teenagers that formed Charlton Athletic in June 1905 found a seemingly permanent home for the club at the Valley, in London, in 1919. However, the club moved to Catford in south east London during 1923 and 1924 and after returning to the Valley, were forced to take up residence with both Crystal Palace and West Ham United between 1985 and 1992. Since that time though, the Valley has indeed been a permanent site for league football for Charlton Athletic Football Club, also known as the Addicks.

The Valley was inaugurated in 1919 and its primary function has been as a football ground, however, it was also home to the London Broncos (now known as Harlequins) for a brief time. When the club first settled at the Valley, funds were tight and many supporters volunteered to prepare the site for matches. The sides were dug out and excavated in order to build up the sides and the original pitch was simply roped-off from spectators who mainly stood to watch their home team. Eventually terraces were installed for the incredibly committed fans who, having worked on their ground, built up an extraordinary relationship with the club. It was, for a long time, the largest League ground in London and had a crowd capacity of around 75,000 in its heyday; the ground's record attendance came in the fifth round of the FA Cup in 1938 against Aston Villa. The supporters' trust acquired the club in 1984 after many years of absence from the top flight, but as was traditional at the Valley, funds were still sadly lacking and the club was forced to move to Selhurst Park when it was unable to accommodate legal requirements to make the ground safer in 1985. It was the first official time that two clubs had shared a football stadium in the League. The club was once again able to own the Valley in 1988 and a huge clean-up operation was launched, however, when a brand new stadium was planned (surrounding the original pitch) they were turned down and fans formed political parties in order to gain seats on the local Greenwich council. It was this move that was instrumental in securing the council's approval of the plans and work began in earnest in 1991.

As a replacement for the covered end, the North Stand increased the ground's capacity to 26,500 following the club's promotion to the Premiership in 2000. It is here that executive boxes and restaurants are housed. The East Stand was built slightly earlier, following the re-opening of the Valley in 1992. Built in 1993 and 1994, the stand also plays host to a number of executive suites. The West Stand, like the East Stand, is two tiered and was constructed in 1998 when Charlton were first promoted to the Premier League. The club's offices and administration are located here along with the directors' box and the boardroom. The players' dressing rooms and conference facilities are also to be found in the West Stand which is also used for official club and community events alike. The South Stand is known as the Jimmy Seed Stand, named for one of the club's first successful managers, and dates from the early 1980s.

RIGHT: The Valley, home of Charlton Athletic since their return from Selhurst Park in 1992.

OPPOSITE: Charlton and Portsmouth fans await their teams' arrival in April 2006.

LEFT: The Barclaycard Premiership match between Charlton Athletic and Everton gets under way at the Valley in August 2001.

CHELSEA

Address:	Stamford Bridge, Fulham Road, London SW6 1HS
Website:	www.chelseafc.com
Ground capacity:	42,055
Pitch dimensions:	103m x 67m
Opened:	1905
Premiership member:	1992-
Record attendance:	82,905 v Arsenal, 12 October 1935, Division One

Located on the "border", between Fulham and Chelsea in west London, lies Stamford Bridge, home of Chelsea. It was sited on Fulham Broadway and built in 1876. Its nickname is "the Bridge" and is, today, the eighth largest ground in the Premier League with a capacity of 42,055. Back in the 1700s, there were two bridges called Standford Bridge (on the Fulham Road and also known as Little Chelsea Bridge) and Stanbridge on the infamous King's Road. It is these bridges, along with Standford Creek that are attributed with giving the original stadium its name.

Stamford Bridge was the original home of the London Athletics Club and opened officially in 1877. The ground was used almost exclusively for athletics until the early 20th century when Joseph Mears and his brother Gus decided that the site was perfect for hosting professional football matches and, in 1905, the New Stamford Bridge stadium was opened in August.

At first the ground was offered to Fulham who turned it down. Chelsea was then founded purposely for the stadium that was designed by the legendary Archie Leitch. Originally, the pitch at the centre of the stadium was surrounded by a running track (maintaining the ground's link with

athletics and keeping it multi-functional as was not unusual). Spectators were mainly housed in the East Stand, although the excavations from the Piccadilly Line construction which was well underway provided steep terracing for those on the west side. As the largest sporting venue in London after Crystal Palace's ground, Stamford Bridge hosted the FA Cup final on a regular basis until the event was moved to Wembley.

A new terrace was added at the south end in 1930 and when part of the area was given a roof it became fondly known as "the Shed". (It was eventually demolished in 1994 and was replaced by an all-seater stand but it is still known as the Shed among fans.) Nine years later, further expansion came with the introduction of seating in the North Stand. This was replaced by open terracing in 1975, but was eventually closed almost 20 years later and two tier seating was erected in what became known as the Matthew Harding Stand. The West Stand was renovated in the mid-1960s but a new and improved stand was built in 1998.

When Stamford Bridge was redeveloped during the 1990s, many new and improved facilities were added including two hotels, bars, restaurants and the Chelsea World of Sport which is an interactive visitor attraction. In 2005, a Club Museum was opened which is also known as the Centenary Museum. More recently, the club announced plans to extend Stamford Bridge to enable a total capacity of 55,000. Due to its current location in London this would prove extremely difficult and so a move away from the ground has become a matter of some speculation. However, the club would not want to have to change its name from Chelsea if it were ever to leave its long-established home at Stamford Bridge.

RIGHT: Chelsea are running out of options as they aim to capitalize on their recent success by extending Stamford Bridge.

Stamford Bridge in 1920. The huge terraced earthworks were a common feature at grounds around the country.

THE MILITARY PICKLE

BEWARE OF PICKPOCKETS

BOX

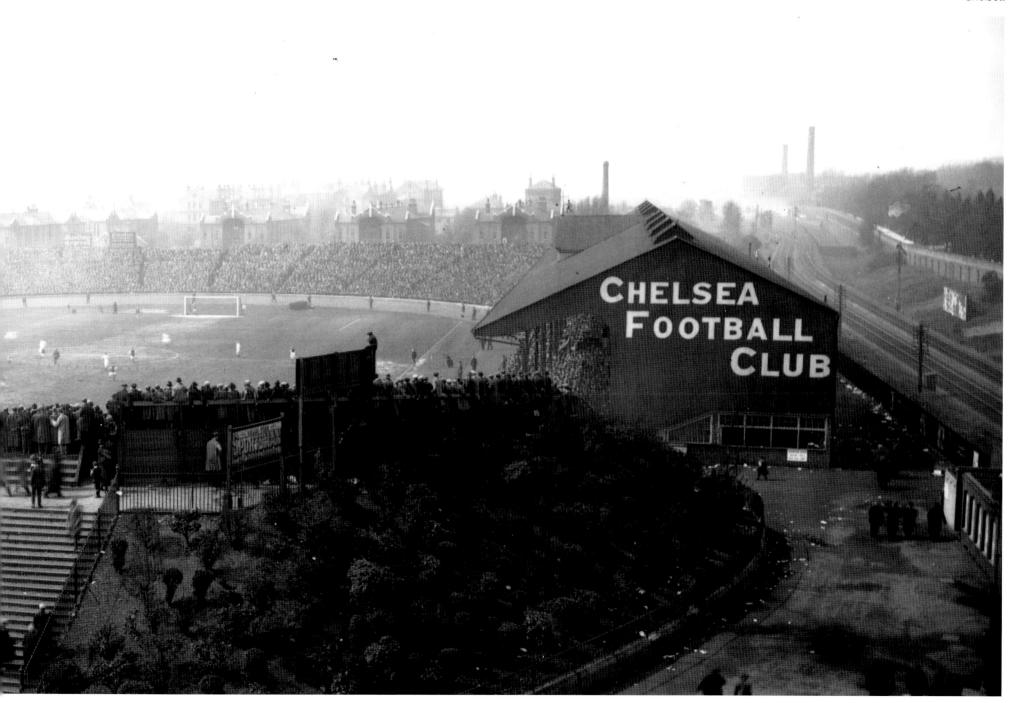

Contrast these two aerial shots of Stamford Bridge taken in 1989 (OPPOSITE) and 2007 (LEFT) and it is easy to see how the ground has been developed.

RIGHT: Chelsea entertain
Manchester City in August 1971
when the ground capacity was
60,000.

OPPOSITE: Stamford Bridge in
February 2008, complete with
warning sign.

COVENTRY CITY

Address:	Ricoh Arena, Phoenix Way, Foleshill, Coventry CV6 6GE
Website:	www.ccfc.co.uk
Ground capacity:	32,609
Pitch dimensions:	101m x 69m
Opened:	2005
Premiership member:	1992-2001
Record attendance:	27,212 v Birmingham City, 31 October 2006, FL Championship

The 32,609 seater stadium, the Ricoh Arena, is home to Coventry City in the Foleshill area of the city. Alongside the stadium itself is an exhibition hall, hotel, leisure club and casino all built on the former site of the Foleshill gasworks. The stadium was opened in 2005 with state of the art facilities and was inaugurated for the start of the 2005-06 season. Unfortunately for the Sky Blues, they had been relegated from the Premiership four years earlier after an unbroken run in the top flight that stretched back to 1967. As it was, the first competitive match at the Ricoh Arena took place against Queens Park Rangers in August 2005. The home side won 3-0 in front of a reduced 23,000 crowd but the first away side to claim victory at the Ricoh Arena was Hull City in a 2-0 triumph over Coventry City just over one month later.

Construction on the ground began in 1999 and was due for completion in 2001, however, the stadium was delayed by four years. It was officially opened by Dame Kelly Holmes and the Sports Minister Richard Caborn on 24 February 2007. With plans to hold a number of rock and pop concerts at the venue, the original plans were for a 45,000 seater stadium, but after a number of unforeseen circumstances, including England's failed bid to host the 2006 World Cup finals, these were downsized.

The sponsorship deal with Ricoh – hence the stadium's name – was reported to be worth more than £10 million and came about after the original sponsor, Jaguar, was forced to pull-out due to financial difficulties. The stadium is run by Arena Coventry Limited, separate from the club itself and is also run as a major concert venue. Top acts to perform at the Ricoh Arena so far have included the likes of Bon Jovi (who is anxious to return to the impressive venue), Bryan Adams and the Red Hot Chili Peppers. The new complex also houses a huge shopping centre which includes the normal expected high street retailers as well as a major superstore, mobile phone and travel stores, a building society, a library and a hairdressers.

Despite the move to the new stadium from their former site of Highfield Road, many critics feel that the Arena is simply too big for the club and attendances have averaged around 50 percent to 60 percent, leaving those in charge disappointed with results. Highfield Road could accommodate 23,600 spectators and it rarely reached capacity.

It hosted its inaugural match in 1899 in the Hillfields area of Coventry and was, at one time, one of the largest playing surfaces in the League and the first all seater stadium in the country. Highfield Road's record attendance came in 1967 when Coventry were playing Wolves in Division Two in front of more than 51,000 spectators. The stadium closed at the end of the 2004-05 season and its final game took place on 30 April 2005 with a 6-2 defeat of rivals Derby County. The last ever goal scored there was by Andrew Whing who began his footballing career in the club's youth academy.

RIGHT: Coventry City's Ricoh Arena has yet to witness Premiership football following the club's 2001 relegation from the top flight.

With a capacity of more than 32,000, the Ricoh Arena is an impressive stadium.

Highfield Road hosts its last game, against Derby County, in April 2005.

CRYSTAL PALACE

Address:	Selhurst Park Stadium, Whitehorse Lane, London SE25 6PU
Website:	www.cpfc.co.uk
Ground capacity:	26,225
Pitch dimensions:	101m x 68m
Opened:	1924
Premiership member:	1992-93, 1994-95, 1997-98, 2004-05
Record attendance:	51,482 v Burnley, 11 May 1979, Division Two

Selhurst Park stadium is located in South Norwood in south London. It is home to Crystal Palace and was designed by Archie Leitch in 1924. As the thirty-first largest stadium in English football the ground has a total capacity today of just over 26,000 and was built on a former brickfield. The site was originally bought for £2,570 from the Brighton Railway Company in 1922 and the ground was completed two years later at a total cost of £30,000. The inaugural match on 30 August 1924 saw Sheffield Wednesday claim a 1-0 victory.

Opened officially by the Lord Mayor of London, the original stadium consisted of one stand and wasn't further developed until 1969 when the club reached the First Division. However, floodlights were installed in 1953 and were replaced by floodlights on pylons in each corner of the ground in 1962. The first team to play at Selhurst Park under the new installations were Real Madrid. It was a major coup for Third Division Palace – it was the visiting team's first match in London.

When renovations did finally begin for the 1969-70 season, the Arthur Wait Stand was added to the Main Stand. Named after the club's former long-standing chairman, the Arthur Wait Stand was constructed as a huge thank you to the man who had often worked on the ground himself and had been instrumental in their rise from the Fourth to the First Division. Next a second tier was added to the Whitehorse Lane End, but the Kop, also known as the Holmesdale Road Terrace needed new facilities to bring it in line with new safety regulations.

In the 1980s, further development came about when the club faced financial difficulties. The rear of the Whitehorse Land End was sold to developers which effectively halved the stand's size and the Main Stand's enclosure was replaced by seating. In 1990, the Arthur Wait Stand's lower half was converted to all-seater following the Taylor Report and executive boxes were added to the roof of the supermarket behind the Whitehorse Lane End which were then roofed and changed to all-seater just over two years later. When Charlton Athletic faced difficulties over renovations of their own ground in 1985 they became the first League club to ground-share with Palace. When Charlton moved back to the Valley, Wimbledon took over the tenancy at Selhurst Park.

In the mid-1990s, the ground underwent additional renovations and the Holmesdale Terrace was replaced with a two tier stand. Wimbledon moved to Milton Keynes in 2003.

The record attendance came in 1979 when more than 51,000 people watched Palace beat Burnley 2-0 in the fight for top place in the Second Division. The 101 mere long pitch (it is 68 metress wide) holds the record for the most number of people watching a League game. In fact, millions watched from the comfort of their own homes in China when Sun Jihai and Fan Zhiyi made their debuts at the ground. They were the first Chinese footballers to play in the English League.

RIGHT: Selhurst Park lies nestled among the terraced housing of Croydon.

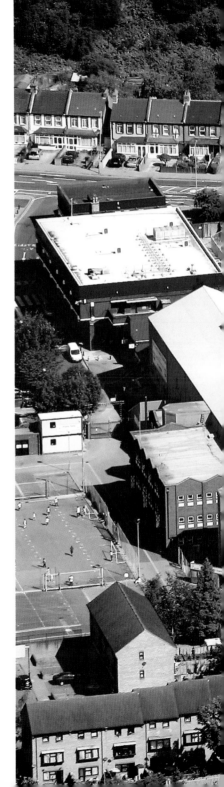

OPPOSITE: Goalmouth action from a foggy Selhurst Park as Palace entertain Sunderland.

LEFT: Selhurst Park, pictured in October 2006, has seen the Eagles groundshare with Charlton Athletic and Wimbledon over the years.

DERBY COUNTY

Address:	Pride Park Stadium, Pride Park, Derby DE24 8XL
Website:	www.dcfc.co.uk
Ground capacity:	33,597
Pitch dimensions:	101m x 68m
Opened:	1997
Premiership member:	1996-2002, 2007-08
Record attendance:	33,475 v Rangers, 1 May 2006, Friendly

It was in the 1880s that foundry owner Francis Ley laid out a sports ground for his employees over a twelve acre area which included football and cricket pitches. Ley, who travelled to the United States, also added a baseball ground to the site and Derby won the English Cup in 1897. By this time, Derby County had made the ground their permanent home following a meeting in 1895 when the club's committee unanimously agreed a move to the site after their continued difficulties staging matches at their previous Racecourse Ground. Ley had already spent £7,000 on improving the ground and agreed to further renovations so that football for the club would have a more workable base. He added six yards to the Normanton Side and a further five yards to the Railway Side and stands were taken from the Racecourse Ground and fixed permanently at the Baseball Ground so that capacity rose from 4,000 to 20,000. When promotion to Division One came in the 1925-26 season major renovations were made to the popular ground.

With the advent of a new stand with seating for more than 3,000 at a cost of £16,000, the Baseball Ground was becoming increasingly high-profile. Players' dressing rooms were now housed in the Main Stand and the crowd capacity was increased to 30,000. A new two tier stand was constructed behind the Normanton goal in the early 1930s but following the Second World War, due to bomb damage, there was talk of moving the club to a newly built stadium. This came to nothing and the Baseball Ground remained Derby County's home until the move to the Pride Park Stadium in July 1997. Further development at the Baseball Ground didn't occur until the late 1960s (although floodlights had been added in the mid-1950s). Due to problems with drainage, the pitch was dug up and replaced and plans were afoot in the 1990s to upgrade the stadium but eventually the Rams decided that a permanent move was preferable.

With a total capacity, today, of 33,597, Pride Park stadium's inaugural match was somewhat of a wash-out. The floodlights in the match against Wimbledon failed part way through and the game was abandoned. There were a number of developments at the stadium during the 2006-07 season. In April, 2007, the club announced the creation of around 250 jobs in the local area with plans for a hotel, bars, restaurants and other facilities, including office space, named the Pride Plaza. The city council were supportive of the redevelopment and on 9 November that same year agreed that the proposal had been successful. The names of club legends such as Brian Clough, Steve Bloomer (the second base baseball player) and Lionel Pickering would all be used for naming a road and two squares within the complex. The club further announced that it had expansion plans for the stadium and would be raising the ground's capacity to 44,000 with work starting at the end of the 2007-08 season. This included adding rows of seats to the North Stand as well as the East and West Stands.

However, it was announced that the increased capacity would be subject to Derby maintaining their Premiership status for the forthcoming 2008-09 season. Unfortunately, this proved to be an impossible task and Derby found themselves going into the Easter programme needing maximum points from their remaining games to avoid relegation. They failed in their task so would kick off 2008-09 in the Championship.

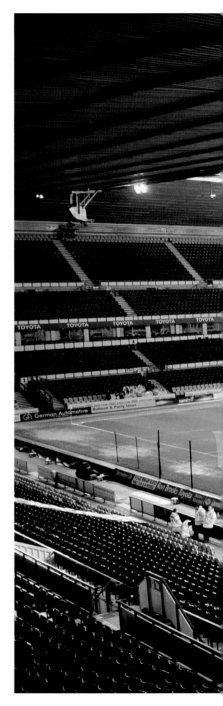

Pride Park in January 2008, a disappointing campaign that saw the Rams relegated.

RIGHT: Pride Park opened in 1997.

OPPOSITE: Derby take on Bolton in December 2001.

LEFT: The Baseball Ground – home to Derby County for more than a century – saw plenty of action. Here, Liverpool are the visitors in a 2-0 home win in January 1975.

EVERTON

Address:	Goodison Park, Goodison Road, Liverpool L4 4EL
Website:	www.evertonfc.com
Ground capacity:	40,394
Pitch dimensions:	100m x 68m
Opened:	1892
Premiership member:	1992-
Record attendance:	78,299 v Liverpool, 18 September 1948, Division One

The home of Everton, Goodison Park was built in 1892 and today has a total capacity of 40,394. It was designed by the Kelly Brothers and built on the former Mere Green Field. Since the site of Everton's home in Liverpool hasn't changed in more than a century, the ground is one of the oldest and most historic of all the Premiership grounds. The ground can also boast being the first ever purpose-built stadium in English football and the first major footballing arena.

Having been driven out of their former home of Anfield when their landlord raised the rent by an extortionate amount in an attempt to cash in on the Toffees winning the League title, land was bought for a little over £8,000 and Goodison Park was officially opened on 24 August 1892. The first stands were uncovered and constructed to hold a total capacity of 8,000 between them. A covered stand was also erected to accommodate a further 3,000 spectators. When development took place, Goodison Park became the first stadium in England to have two tier stands on all four sides and was nicknamed "The Grand Old Lady". It made history again when it became the first football ground to have a three tier stand and King George V became the first reigning monarch to attend a football match here in 1913.

Dugouts – which originated from the Dons' trainer, Donald Coleman in Scotland – were then the added at Goodison, making Everton the first English club to utilize them in 1931. Goodison Park then went on to host more international matches than any other English ground. The four stands today include: the Park End, with a capacity of 6,000; Bullens Road (capacity 8,067); Gwladys Street End with a capacity of 10,155; and the Main Stand which accommodates more than 16,300 spectators. Backing on to Walton Lane, the Park End stand was completed in 1994 and consists of a single tier to the south of the ground. Bullens Road was designed by Archie Leitch and is a two tier building on the east side of the pitch divided into three areas; the Paddock and Upper and Lower Bullens. Gwladys Street End was also designed by the legendary Scot and is situated behind the goal at the north end of Goodison. The Main Stand is three tier and was completed in the early 1970s.

Although Goodison could have further renovations and could effectively undergo expansion, the club do not think the plans are financially viable. Therefore, there were plans afoot for Everton to move from their current ground to a proposed site at King's Dock. After four years of debate, with serious opposition from the supporters' group, the Goodison Forever-ton (GFE), there seemed little chance of resolving the issue. However, 85 percent of supporters voted in favour of a move but plans fell through when Everton failed to gain the necessary financial backing. Stanley Park (a purpose-built stadium) was proposed as a permanent home for both Liverpool and Everton but both clubs rejected the idea.

It left Everton – who tasted Champions League football for the first time in 2005-06 courtesy of their fourth place finish in the Premiership – with the difficult decision of whether to try and move to a new site and develop their own stadium, or whether to go back to the drawing board and look, once again, at plans to renovate the current site at Goodison Park.

It is plain to see, with Goodison Park being encompassed by houses, why Everton have considered building a new stadium on a different site.

RIGHT: *Fans congregate outside Goodison Park for a match against Birmingham City in August 2002.*

OPPOSITE: *The interior of a packed Goodison Park.*

Left: Policeman Sid Palmer and his Alsatian Cindy watch the groundsman prepare the Goodison Park pitch during a World Cup security patrol before the Brazil v Bulgaria match on 12 July 1966.

OPPOSITE: The stands began to fill as Everton entertain Spurs.

LEFT: Jubilation at Goodison in the October 2007 Merseyside derby as Sami Hyypia scores an own goal.

FULHAM

Address:	Craven Cottage, Stevenage Road, London SW6 6HH
Website:	www.fulhamfc.co.uk
Ground capacity:	26,600
Pitch dimensions:	100m x 67m
Opened:	1896
Premiership member:	2001-
Record attendance:	49,335 v Millwall, 8 October 1938, Division Two

Situated on the Stevenage Road in the Hammersmith and Fulham area of London is Craven Cottage, home to Fulham since 1896. The six acre site was designed by Archie Leitch and today has a total capacity of 26,600 with plans to increase this to 30,500 over coming seasons.

The original "Cottage" was built in 1780 by William Craven, and the surrounding areas were made up of the hunting land of Anne Boleyn, wife of King Henry VIII. Many other sporting events took place around the Cottage until it was destroyed by fire in 1888 and subsequently abandoned. Including Loftus Road, Fulham have had nine previous homes before they moved to Craven Cottage permanently.

In 1894, the land that Fulham chose for their new ground was so overgrown that it took two years for the site to be even vaguely usable for football. The first game which accepted paying spectators took place in October 1896 and the first real development was the construction of a stand shortly after. When the local council tried to shut the ground over safety concerns, Archie Leitch was hired to design a new stadium. The pavilion (the Cottage) and a further stand were built and, along with the Johnny Haynes Stand (renamed after the tragic death of the firm Fulham

favourite and former England captain), are now Grade II listed buildings. The ground established itself as a first class stadium from the beginning but it wasn't until the club reached top flight football in 1949 that improvements were made. In 1950, floodlights were added, an electronic scoreboard was introduced and the Hammersmith End was roofed.

The Riverside Terracing (which enabled fans to turn around and watch the Oxford versus Cambridge boat race) was replaced by the Eric Miller Stand in the 1970s. After the former director's suicide, the stand became better known as the Riverside Stand. For four years in the early 1980s, the stadium was also home to the Fulham Rugby League side who went on to become the London Broncos (now the Harlequins).

Following the Taylor Report, Craven Cottage still had standing areas in 2002 and no plans to replace these will seats. The club played their home games at Loftus Road and a pressure group was formed to encourage the powers that be that Craven Cottage needed renovating. Eventually, Fulham returned to the Cottage for the 2004-05 season where the less than "state of the art" stadium could do with some improvements to bring it into the 21st century, despite its fine architecture.

To the north of the pitch is the Hammersmith (or Hammy) End while the Putney End sits to the south. To the right of the stand is the Cottage and Bishop's Park, where fans in earlier times used to sneak into the ground where they paid "boot" money – they placed their money for the game in the players' boots. It is also here that Fulham have a special license from the FA to have a designated neutral area. This came about because of the fans' impeccable behaviour and they are the only Premiership side to have an area for this purpose. The Riverside Stand, as its name suggests, backs on to the Thames while the former Stevenage Road Stand (now the Johnny Haynes Stand) was named after the road it ran alongside.

Since Mohamed Al Fayed took over as chairman, the club have reached the Premiership but fight a perennial battle against the drop.

A splash of colour in an otherwise grim sky over Craven Cottage in March 2007.

RIGHT: *Wilfred Bouma (Aston Villa)*
and Simon Davies compete for the
ball with the famous Cottage in the
background.

OPPOSITE: Match stewards watch
the action as Fulham take on
Blackburn Rovers in December
2005.

OPPOSITE: An aerial shot of Craven Cottage. Before the Riverside Terrace was replaced, fans used to be able to simultaneously watch the Boat Race and the Cottagers.

OPPOSITE: Happy days for Fulham manager Chris Coleman as he watches his side beat West Brom 6-1 in February 2006.

RIGHT: In scenes that would not be seen in today's Premiership, a groundsman ensures the pitch markings are clear of snow as Fulham play Everton in January 1926.

OPPOSITE: Craven Cottage has been developed over the years within its geographical restrictions and now boasts a capacity of approximately 25,000.

IPSWICH TOWN

Address:	Portman Road, Ipswich, Suffolk IP1 2DA
Website:	www.itfc.co.uk
Ground capacity:	30,311
Pitch dimensions:	102m x 66m
Opened:	1884
Premiership member:	1992-95, 2000-02
Record attendance:	38,010 v Leeds United, 8 March 1975, FA Cup

Based in the town itself is Ipswich Town's home, Portman Road, owned by Suffolk County Council. The club have been resident here since 1884 when the stadium was opened and shared it with East Suffolk Cricket Club who used the ground during the summer months. The first permanent building was actually a cricket pavilion and further, more substantial, developments didn't materialize until the mid-1890s.

As an amateur side, Ipswich didn't require any real "stadium-like" facilities, however, when Aston Villa visited the ground in 1898 a temporary stand was erected to house 5,000 spectators. The first permanent stand followed in 1906 at the Portman Road side and during the First World War the site was used as an army training camp. When the club returned to the ground two years after the end of the war, the grass had to be repaired substantially, due to the heavy machinery that had been used by the army.

When the club turned professional in 1936, the cricket club were moved out and the first bank of terracing was created at the north end of the pitch. The Supporters' Association were instrumental in funding a number of developments at the site and, in 1952, concrete terracing

replaced the wooden ones and the North Stand was re-terraced two years later. Later into the decade, the West Stand was constructed and floodlights were added in 1959; all thanks to the efforts of the supporters. Television cameras arrived in 1962 and were followed by *Match of the Day* six years later. Developments were ongoing and dressing rooms were built in the mid-1960s. The club signed a 99 year lease as tenants in 1968.

Advertising hoards appeared around the ground in the early 1970s for the first time and the "Centre Spot", a restaurant under the Portman Stand, underwent construction. The ground's record attendance of 38,010 came in 1975 in the FA Cup tie with Leeds United, but following success in the 1978 FA Cup when they beat Arsenal 1-0 at Wembley, twenty four executive boxes were added in front of the Portman Stand. However, following new safety regulations, the capacity in front of these boxes was reduced when seating was introduced.

The Tractor Boys won the Second Division title at the right time and were founder members of the Premiership but this lasted status just three seasons. When Ipswich returned to the top flight in 2000, further investment into the stadium was made at a cost of £22 million. Both the North and South Stands were renovated and in 2001 sponsorship came in the guise of brewery Greene King, and the South Stand was renamed in recognition of this support. The other two stands are the Cobbold Stand (originally the Portman Stand) and the Britannia Stand. All four stands are covered and multi-tiered.

Portman Road has also hosted a number of international fixtures (including a senior England friendly against Croatia and several youth internationals) and has been used for rock and pop concerts with performances by Sir Elton John, REM, the Red Hot Chili Peppers, Rod Stewart, Dire Straits and Neil Diamond among others. The current capacity of Portman Road is 30,311 around this 102 metre long and 66 metre wide pitch.

Portman Road has been home to Ipswich Town since 1884.

RIGHT: The exterior of Portman Road and the training pitch.

OPPOSITE: George Burley is unveiled as Ipswich manager in May 2001.

LEEDS UNITED

Address:	Elland Road, Leeds, West Yorkshire LS11 0ES
Website:	www.leedsunited.com
Ground capacity:	39,419
Pitch dimensions:	105m x 68m
Opened:	1919
Premiership member:	1992-2004
Record attendance:	57,892 v Sunderland, 15 March 1967, FA Cup

Built and opened in 1897, Elland Road, home of Leeds United is the eleventh largest football stadium in England. It was used for Rugby League but turned its sporting attentions to football when the ground was purchased by Leeds City in 1904. However, the newly formed club faced a number of financial difficulties over the next decade and the FA took possession of the stadium in 1919.

Despite a lack of affordable housing in the area, when the council bought the ground they allowed Leeds United (who formed in the aftermath of Leeds City's demise) to become tenants until such time that they could buy it themselves. Although the club did eventually buy the stadium, over the following years a number of problems with finance led to the ground being purchased a number of times and to this day, Leeds United are still tenants. However, in March 2007, the chief executive, Shaun Harvey, announced that the club had been in negotiations with Leeds City Council to help them buy Elland Road once again along with Thorp Arch.

The South Stand (also known as the scratching shed) was constructed in 1971 and until the Taylor Report consisted of standing room only on the lower tier. This was replaced by seating in 1993. The West Stand was destroyed by a huge fire in September 1956 and a public appeal raised half the money to replace the original construction. The new West Stand was opened in August 1957 while the conference centre and other facilities were opened in 1991. The East Stand, with its seating for 17,000 spectators was opened during the 1992-93 season and, at the time, was the largest cantilever construction in the world. Just two seasons later and the Don Revie Stand (the Kop) was refurbished. The television gantry is located in the West Stand for covering both domestic matches and the internationals that have been held here. A number of England internationals have been hosted by Elland Road while Rugby League has also enjoyed the facilities of this stadium. Indeed, the Hunslet Hawks had a temporary base here and the stadium was chosen for the Rugby League Tri-Nations final in both 2004 and 2005.

Like other sporting venues, Elland Road has been a firm favourite among the concert fraternity and a number of bands have performed here. In 1982, Queen became the first band to gig at the stadium and were followed by U2 in 1987. The Happy Mondays live album in 1991 was performed here and remains popular with top artists into the 21st century; in May 2008 the Kaiser Chiefs chose the venue for their live performance.

In 2001 plans were afoot to either move the club to a newer stadium at Skelton or look at improving the capacity and facilities at Elland Road. However, money was once again on the agenda. It transpired that the club had rising debts which coupled, with relegation from the Premiership in 2004, did little to ensure a move to new premises. Elland Road, it seemed, would have to suffice.

When Ken Bates became chairman, he was adamant that improvements to the stadium could be made once the club was back in top flight football. Sadly, a further relegation to the former Division Three meant that the Elland Road faithful would have to wait a while longer. The main plan at the current time is to buy back the stadium from the council.

The end of the dream for Leeds United as a 3-3 draw with Charlton in May 2004 is not enough to secure their Premiership survival.

OPPOSITE: Elland Road has witnessed many ups and downs, but the lowest was when the club was relegated to the third tier of English football in May 2007.

LEFT: A hearse carries the legendary John Charles into the stadium for his memorial service in March 2004.

LEICESTER CITY

Address:	The Walkers Stadium, Filbert Way, Leicester LE2 7FL
Website:	www.lcfc.co.uk
Ground capacity:	32,312
Pitch dimensions:	100m x 68m
Opened:	2002
Premiership member:	1994-95, 1996-2002, 2003-04
Record attendance:	32,148 v Newcastle United, 26 December 2003, Premier League

The Walkers Stadium, an all-seater ground which was opened in 2002 by former Foxes striker Gary Lineker, is home to Leicester City. It is situated on Filbert Way nestling along the banks of the Grand Union Canal in Leicester. The 32,500 capacity stadium held its inaugural match in July the year it opened and is named after Walkers crisps who signed a 10-year sponsorship with the club. The Walkers Stadium cost a total of £37 million but, at the time, things were proving difficult for Leicester who had just gone into receivership. However, a US firm, Teachers Insurance provided £28 million in a deal which allowed the club to remain as tenants in their new stadium on a long-term lease.

The first three goals scored by Leicester players at the new stadium came courtesy of Jordan Stewart in a 1-1 draw friendly against Athletic Bilbao and Brian Deane who netted the ball twice in a 2-0 victory over Watford in the stadium's first competitive game. After claiming second place in the First Division table at the end of the 2002-03 season, Leicester reclaimed their place in the top flight and the Walkers Stadium became part of the Premiership's history.

The new stadium had been deemed necessary during the 1990s for several reasons. First, football was becoming ever more popular and, second, it was decided that Leicester City had outgrown their original site on Filbert Street. In addition, the previous stadium was badly in need of redevelopment. After a plan to develop a site at Bede Island South failed, Freemans Wharf – the site of a former power station – close to Filbert Street was chosen and planning permission granted. Twenty-two acres of industrial land was used to design and construct the Walkers Stadium by the Miller Partnership who worked on the project between June 2001 and the stadium's opening in July 2002. But Filbert Street, the first official ground of Leicester City, remains dear to club and supporters alike. Between 1891 and 2002, the City Business Stadium – as it was officially known – was home to the club formerly known as Leicester Fosse. Leicester Fosse moved to Filbert Street in 1891 having already had five previous "homes". The stadium began as earth banks adjacent to a small main stand situated on the west side but in 1921 a much larger stand was constructed. Six years later and an even bigger stand was erected at the south end which was fondly known as the "double decker".

Like most other Premiership clubs and grounds, Leicester City found no escape from the Second World War and the main stand suffered substantial bomb damage in 1940. This was further compounded by a serious fire, but German prisoners of war provided much of the labour needed to reconstruct the stadium and capacity reached 42,000 by 1949. At its peak, the stadium reached a maximum capacity of 47,298 but this was reduced by Filbert Street's closure date to 22,000 with the removal of terraces. The final game played at the stadium was a fitting tribute to the site when Leicester City defeated Tottenham Hotspur 2-1 at the end of the 2001-02 season bringing 111 years of tradition to an end. By 2003, Filbert Street had been demolished and has subsequently been developed as the Filbert Village which houses students of De Montfort University and Leicester University where the main thoroughfare running through the site is aptly named Lineker Road.

The Walkers Stadium boasts a capacity of 32,500.

RIGHT: The finishing touches are added to the Walkers Stadium.

OPPOSITE: The Walkers Stadium, pictured in July 2002.

RIGHT: *The exterior of Filbert Street, the home of Leicester City from 1891 until 2002.*

OPPOSITE: *The final game at Filbert Street saw Leicester City triumph 2-1 over Tottenham Hotspur during a Premiership match on 11 May 2002.*

LIVERPOOL

Address:	Anfield, Anfield Road, Liverpool L4 0TH
Website:	www.liverpoolfc.tv
Ground capacity:	45,362
Pitch dimensions:	101m x 68m
Opened:	1892
Premiership member:	1992-
Record attendance:	61,905 v Wolverhampton Wanderers, 2 February 1952, FA Cup

Anfield has been home to Liverpool since the club's formation in 1892 when rivals Everton moved to Goodison Park. It has a capacity of 45,362 where fans and away supporters alike can watch the exciting action on the 101 metre by 68 metre pitch.

There are four stands at Anfield comprising the Spion Kop, the Main Stand, Anfield Road and the Centenary Stand. As with all other large clubs, the ground's record attendance was noted prior to the Taylor Report (amongst others), when spectator safety became paramount. In Liverpool's case, the largest attendance was recorded in 1952 when 61,905 fans turned out to see the FA Cup tie against Wolverhampton Wanderers.

Liverpool joined the Football League a year after moving to Anfield and a new stand for 3,000 spectators was built in 1895. It was constructed on the site of the now Main Stand and was continually developed until it was replaced in 1973. Local sports journalist and editor Ernest Jones named the Spion Kop – a name that has stuck ever since – and was further developed in 1928. Floodlights were installed in the mid-1950s. The four stands are now all-seater and are covered, however, only the Anfield Road End and the Centenary Stand (which was originally the Kemlyn Road Stand) are multi-tiered.

Anfield has a Hillsborough memorial which is situated by the Shankly gates. It is a permanent reminder of the 96 people who died during the 1989 FA Cup semi-final at Hillsborough and is always decorated with flowers and tributes. The centre of the memorial is an eternal flame. The stadium also recognises two of the club's most successful managers, Bob Paisley and Bill Shankly. Both men have gates at the stadium named after them in tribute while Bill Shankly is also honoured with a bronze statue which is found in front of the visitors' centre by the Kop.

As well as Premiership football, Anfield has also hosted a number of other events including FA Cup semi-finals, senior international matches and boxing. The latter activity was a regular feature at the stadium between the First and Second World Wars. Other sports hosted here include professional tennis where Fred Perry, the Wimbledon and US Open champion was always a favourite with the crowds. It was also the finish line in the Liverpool marathon during the 1920s.

The stadium is a UEFA four star ground and has been the venue of numerous international matches but in 2011 the club are hoping to move to Stanley Park which will accommodate an additional 15,000 fans. The original plans for a replacement stadium were outlined in 2002. Despite Liverpool Council's attempts to move both Liverpool and Everton to the new proposed site at Stanley Park, both clubs firmly declined a ground-sharing opportunity.

Planning permission was granted in July 2004 and the local council agreed a 999 year lease on the site . Following the club's takeover in early 2007 – although tensions mounted between the two main shareholders in April 2008 – Stanley Park was redesigned and the council gave the go-ahead for the 60,000 seater project towards the end of that same year.

RIGHT: Turnstile operators await their instructions before the game with Newcastle in September 2006.

Two images that will forever be associated with Anfield: the immortal "You'll Never Walk Alone" adorns the Shankly Gate (OPPOSITE); and a packed Kop in September 2007 (LEFT).

RIGHT: Always a place visiting teams fear...despite the obvious "welcome".

OPPOSITE: Liverpool legend Kevin Keegan is pictured on the Anfield terracing in March 1976.

With Anfield (OPPOSITE) suffering from similar "overcrowding" to nearby Goodison Park, plans were announced in July 2007 for a new 60,000 all-seater stadium (LEFT).

MANCHESTER CITY

Address:	City of Manchester Stadium, SportCity, Manchester M11 3FF
Website:	www.mcfc.co.uk
Ground capacity:	47,726
Pitch dimensions:	105m x 68m
Opened:	2003
Premiership member:	1992-96, 2000-01, 2002-
Record attendance:	47,304 v Chelsea, 28 February 2004, Premier League

For 80 years, Maine Road situated in Moss Side in Manchester was home to Manchester City. Construction at Maine Road was first announced in 1922 when City decided to leave their earlier ground at Hyde Road; it had been badly damaged by fire in 1920 and had little room for expansion. Many fans were disappointed with the proposed new site at Maine Road as they felt that the club had its roots firmly in the east of the city. The architect that eventually won fans over was Charles Swain and a total capacity of 80,000 was granted which dubbed the new stadium "the Wembley of the North". But construction wasn't without its problems. Gypsies had originally inhabited the site and it was said that a curse was placed on the land when the occupants were requested to leave.

The first match at Maine Road came in August 1923 in front of a well attended crowed. Nearly 57,000 spectators turned out to watch City beat Sheffield United in a 2-1 victory. Then, in 1931, development between the corner of the Main Stand and the Platt Lane End took place and a roof was added to the construction. Maine Road also holds the record for the highest number of spectators to watch any type of football match in England when more than 84,500 people attended a game between the home side and Stoke City in the sixth round of the FA Cup in 1934.

But, change was imminent and, in 2003, Manchester City moved to the newly built City of Manchester Stadium. The purpose-built sporting facility had been constructed when the 2002 Commonwealth Games were to be held in the city following a failed bid to host the 2000 Summer Olympics. The stadium was opened to athletics on 25 July 2002.

Designed by Arup Associates, the stadium was converted to a football stadium following the Games and City signed a 250 year lease. The actual stadium is bowl-shaped and has a seating capacity of 47,726 making it the fifth largest stadium in the Premiership and the twelfth largest in the UK. The continuous oval interior (with three tier seating at the sides and two tier seating at either end) has a total of 68 executive boxes which are located along the North, East and West Stands. Despite its continuity, each side of the stadium has its own name and the final "stand" is, of course, named the South Stand.

The pitch is also unique in that it is the widest in English football and the grass is reinforced with artificial grass fibres while the roof is suspended from steel cables attached to eight towers. With ventilation to the pitch assured through areas in each "corner" without seating, its impressive modern look and well thought out design, the stadium has won several awards including the RIBA Inclusive Design Award (2004) and the Institution of Structural Engineers Special Award in 2003.

Although City have suffered two relegations from the Premiership (in 1996 and 2001), the blue half of Manchester have been forced to live in their neighbours' shadows as nine titles were claimed by the Old Trafford outfit. The 2007-08 season, however, looked to offer a reversal in fortunes with City making a fantastic start to the campaign but they could not keep the pace going and dropped to a mid-table position.

RIGHT: Built for the 2002 Commonwealth Games, the City of Manchester Stadium has hosted Premiership football since August 2003.

RIGHT: New signings Antoine Sibierski (left) and Trevor Sinclair are unveiled in August 2003.

OPPOSITE: The stadium's impressive entrance in June 2007.

LEFT: *The facilities at City's new stadium are far better than the club enjoyed at Maine Road.*

Maine Road in the 1970s.

Manchester City's last game at Maine Road saw them lose 1-0 to Southampton on 11 May 2003.

MANCHESTER UNITED

Address:	Old Trafford, Sir Matt Busby Way,
	Manchester M16 0RA
Website:	www.manutd.com
Ground capacity:	76,212
Pitch dimensions:	105m x 68m
Opened:	1910
Premiership member:	1992-
Record attendance:	76,098 v Blackburn Rovers,
	31 March 2007, Premier League

Located on the aptly named Sir Matt Busby Way, Old Trafford in Greater Manchester, "The Theatre of Dreams" – as it was nicknamed by Sir Bobby Charlton – is the home of Manchester United. Designed by renowned architect Archibald Leitch, Old Trafford has been the club's residence since 1910. It is the largest Premiership ground in the country and is an all-seater stadium which has hosted some of the most memorable games in English football history. It is also the twelfth largest stadium in Europe and the thirty-sixth largest football venue in the world.

Despite the club's absence from the ground between 1941 and 1949 due to bomb damage during the Second World War, the stadium has remained a constant for club and fans alike and lies close to Old Trafford cricket ground. The actual pitch is around nine inches higher than the surrounding grassed areas which ensures adequate drainage of surface water. The grass is cut three times a week during the spring and summer and once a week over the autumn and winter. The Manchester United Club Museum is set in the North Stand and attracts a phenomenal 200,000 visitors ever year.

Before the early 1900s, United were known as Newton Heath and had a home in Clayton on Bank Street, but near-bankruptcy brought about a change of name to Manchester United. The same situation also saw refinancing at the club and a new stadium was built at a cost of 60,000. Completed in 1909 by Leitch, the first match at Old Trafford – where the South Stand was covered for the first time – saw rivals Liverpool beat United 4-3. The following years were ground-breaking at Old Trafford where the FA Cup final was played in 1911 and 1915.

The events of the Second World War saw the destruction of much of the stadium, particularly the Main Stand, on 11 March 1941. It was rebuilt eight years later and followed by various redevelopments which included covering all the stands. The stadium also received floodlighting but further reconstruction during the 1950s saw more modern architecture in the creation of a bowl-style ground. When the United Road or North Stand was unveiled in 1964, it was the first time in football history that private boxes were offered. The canted roof was then extended along the seating to the scoreboard before work began on the South Stand. Most recent developments include an additional 8,000 seats located in a second tier of the north west and north east corners of the stadium. The only single tiered stand is the South which has a railway line behind it. If difficulties in building over the line and other issues could be addressed, a second tier on the South Stand could take the stadium's capacity to more than 95,500.

The stadium has been a popular venue for film-makers since the early 1960s and became the first ground to use a perimeter fence to guard against violence and hooliganism amongst fans. The stadium made even more history in March 2006 when its capacity attendance reached 69,070 setting a record in the Premiership. But subsequent matches have seen United play to even bigger audiences and almost exactly a year after setting the record, the Old Trafford – the only UEFA 5 star rated facility in the country – played host to 76,098 supporters.

An aerial view of Old Trafford ahead of the Premiership match against Reading on 30 December 2006.

RIGHT: The Stretford End was
converted into all-seater stand in
time for the 1993-94 season.

OPPOSITE: United commemorate
the 50th anniversary of the
Munich crash in February 2008.

A panoramic view of the interior of Old Trafford in November 2003.

Old Trafford in the 1930s (RIGHT), with its earthwork terracing on three sides of the ground, is a far cry from the 21st century stadium (OPPOSITE) that boasts a capacity of more than 76,000.

MIDDLESBROUGH

Address:	Riverside Stadium,
	Middlesbrough TS3 6RS
Website:	www.mfc.co.uk
Ground capacity:	35,041
Pitch dimensions:	105m x 68m
Opened:	1995
Premiership member:	1992-93, 1995-97, 1998-
Record attendance:	34,836 v Norwich City,
	28 December 2004, Premier League

Middlesbrough moved to the Riverside Stadium when its doors opened in August 1995 with a capacity of 35,100. It was built specifically in line with recommendations in the Taylor Report and was the largest new football ground to be constructed since the Second World War. Ayresome Park, the club's former ground, was unsuitable for expansion due to its location in a residential area and the site at Middlehaven on the River Tees was offered for the proposed stadium.

When Middlesbrough was first formed, their home ground was Linthorpe Road. However, the club's promotion to the Football League in 1893 meant that a larger and improved stadium was needed and Ayresome Park was built just across from the old ground at Paradise Field. The new ground was opened in 1903 and it became high-profile during the FIFA World Cup in 1966 when three games were staged at Ayresome Park.

By the early 1990s, the stadium had simply seen better days and major renovations were needed in order to take the stadium into the 21st century. In addition, the Taylor Report put paid to any hope Middlesbrough had of Ayresome Park hosting top flight games. The final game at the stadium came on 30 April 1995 against Luton Town where the home side claimed a 2-1 victory. It was fitting that the club's campaign had earned

promotion to the Premiership for what would be their first season at the newly constructed Riverside Stadium. In 1997, Ayresome Park was demolished and houses were erected in its place. However, to maintain a link with its past, the club took the gates from Ayresome Park and these were installed at the new stadium's main entrance.

The name Riverside Stadium was chosen by fans; among other choices were Middlehaven Stadium, Erimus Stadium and Teesside Stadium. The first game played at the new ground was against Chelsea on 26 August 1995 and Middlesbrough won 2-1. It was a fitting start to their Premiership campaign with goals by Craig Hignett and Jan Aage Fjortoft.

To date, the ground's record attendance came on 11 June 2003 when 35,000 spectators watched England versus Slovakia in a Euro 2004 qualifier. For the club itself, the next highest recorded attendance happened on 28 December the following year, in a match against Norwich City which was watched by 34,836 fans.

The Euro 2004 qualifier was the first – and so far – the only senior international hosted at the stadium. England won the match 2-1 with goals by Michael Owen when Slovakia were leading while, in the stadium's first year, the England Under-21s met Brazil in a match that featured the up and coming David Beckham for the home side and Ronaldinho for the visitors. In terms of the future, planning permission has already been granted should the club wish to expand the current capacity up to 42,000.

Though Boro failed to consolidate their status as a Premiership side at the first two times of asking, they have remained in the top flight since 1998 and claimed their first major piece of silverware with the 2004 League Cup. This also paved the way for the club's first ever foray into European competition.

RIGHT: The Riverside Stadium in March 2008.

LEFT: The Riverside Stadium has been home to Middlesbrough since 1995.

RIGHT AND OPPOSITE: The impressive Riverside Stadium is more than a match for its much newer contemporaries.

RIGHT: *The perfectly-manicured surface of the Riverside Stadium pitch, where more than 35,000 can watch the game in comfort.*

OPPOSITE: *A scramble in the goalmouth during North Korea's World Cup match against Italy at Ayresome Park on 19 July 1966.*

MILTON KEYNES DONS

Address:	Stadium:mk, Way West, Milton Keynes MK1 1ST
Website:	www.mkdons.com
Ground capacity:	22,000
Pitch dimensions:	105m x 68m
Opened:	2007
Premiership member:	1992-2000 (as Wimbledon)
Record attendance:	14,521 v Peterborough United, 21 March 2008, Division Two

Located in Denbigh, Milton Keynes, Stadium:mk is home to the Milton Keynes Dons who moved to the ground in November 2007. The complex is designed mostly for football matches and comprises the Arena:MK – an indoor facility which is home to the Marshall Milton Keynes Lions professional basketball team as of 2008 – and the Desso GrassMaster pitch. Designed by HOK SVE and constructed by the Buckingham Group, the multi-purpose stadium is state of the art with a total capacity of 22,000, although there are plans in place to increase this by 10,000 at some point in the future (probably within twelve to eighteen months of opening). At present, the current capacity crowd are accommodated in the lower tier only.

Wimbledon had stunned the footballing world with their progress as a professional club. They only joined the Football League in 1977 yet within nine years had earned their place in the top flight. An FA Cup final followed in 1988 and the underdogs scored a surprise win over Liverpool with a single Lawrie Sanchez goal. Sadly, the Crazy Gang's top flight adventure came to an end with relegation in 2000. The Dons had been forced to move from their Plough Lane home and began a ground-share with Crystal Palace at Selhurst Park in 1991 before officially moving to the

National Hockey Stadium twelve years later. The original plans were for the club's new stadium to open in time for the 2004-05 season, however, it would take another three years before the purpose-built facilities were ready. While waiting for their new stadium to be completed, Wimbledon (having no connection with the area in south London anymore) made the bold decision to change the club's name. Milton Keynes Dons was the preferred choice.

The stadium was officially opened by Queen Elizabeth II on 29 November 2007 and has been carefully designed to meet with UEFA's Elite Stadium specifications. Despite the official opening, the first competitive game at Stadium:mk took place some months earlier in July 2007 in a match against Chelsea. The Dons claimed victory in a 4-3 win. That same month, the stadium hosted a particularly special match between England players and other sporting legends from around the world in memory of the late Alan Ball, the legendary England midfielder.

Milton Keynes is particularly renowned for its concrete cows among other things and when the fans first encountered the South Stand it quickly became known as the cowshed.

The first international match took place towards the end of 2007 when the England Under-21 team met Bulgaria in a UEFA Euro 2009 qualifying round. The stadium then found itself with a very different role when it became the focal point for Milton Keynes's fortieth birthday celebrations.

The Stadium:mk also has exceptional hotel and conference facilities while the ballroom is the largest conference, or venue, facility in the south east of England outside London. Up to 1,000 guests can easily be accommodated in the expansive room. Equally impressive is the four star hotel which has some rooms with a pitch-view facility that can be converted for matches. There are many advertising and sponsorship opportunities for corporate businesses as well as a club shop which sells everything from kits and accessories and gifts.

LEFT: Stadium:mk has been home to the Milton Keynes Dons since 2007 following their four-year stay at the National Hockey Stadium.

ABOVE: Of course, as Wimbledon, the Dons played their Premiership games at Crystal Palace's Selhurst Park.

NEWCASTLE UNITED

Address:	St James' Park, Newcastle-upon-Tyne NE1 4ST
Website:	www.nufc.co.uk
Ground capacity:	52,387
Pitch dimensions:	105m x 68m
Opened:	1892
Premiership member:	1993-
Record attendance:	68,386 v Chelsea, 3 September 1930, Division One

The 52,387 capacity all-seater stadium in Newcastle-upon-Tyne in the north of England is home to Newcastle United, nicknamed the Magpies. St James' Park has been at the centre of many highs and lows during its long established history which began in 1892. Like many other older-style stadiums, St James' Park is at the heart of the city, and with its distinctive white cantilever roof, it is clearly across the Newcastle skyline.

Fans at St James' are known as the Toon Army and first came to prominence when Newcastle East End and Newcastle West End joined forces to form the current club. Although football began at the site in 1880, it wasn't until twelve years later than Newcastle United took up its permanent residence at the ground. Little changed over subsequent years, until demands for better safety (in line with every other English club) came about in the early 1990s. Although it was no fault of the club's, three supporters had tried tunnelling their way under the ground in 1958 so that they could play on the pitch at night. Five days later the tunnel collapsed and two of the men were killed. However, it was the advent of the Hillsborough disaster that brought about the greatest changes when it became a requirement that all stadiums become all-seated.

As a result, it was suggested that Newcastle should relocate to Leazes Park where a new purpose-built stadium would replace St James', while the old ground seemed destined to become home to the Falcons Rugby Club.

However, the ambitious plans fell through when a conservation group launched a protest and it was decided to expand the current site by incorporating additional tiers to two existing stands; the Sir John Hall Stand and the Milburn Stand. In further renovations the East Stand was redeveloped to mirror the Milburn Stand and upper tiers in the North and West sides were constructed complete with executive boxes. More recently, the Gallowgate End was redeveloped in 2005 and includes a bar named "Shearer's" after Newcastle favourite Alan Shearer. Also incorporated into the Gallowgate End was a new club shop, a museum and box office.

In April 2007, further expansion plans were announced which would total £300 million to develop the stadium and the surrounding area. The proposal was to add a major conference centre, hotels and luxury apartments and to further renovate the Gallowgate End but the plans became uncertain when the club was taken over by Mike Ashley. There are already conference and banqueting facilities at St James' while the Milburn Stand has premium seating (arranged in private clubs) which all have access to their own bar and lounge.

Any future plans to expand at St James' could well take the total capacity of 52,387 up to 60,000. However, despite the club's lack of form in recent years it is already the third largest Premiership ground (after the Emirates Stadium and Old Trafford) and is the seventh largest football stadium in the UK. The return of Kevin Keegan – nicknamed "the Messiah" for his previous achievements at the club – as manager was welcomed with great euphoria in January 2008.

Although the stadium resembles most large footballing arenas, St James' is unique for its lack of scoreboard.

St James' Park was chosen as one of the venues for Euro '96.

RIGHT: Preparations are under way for the pitch to be relaid.

Newcastle take on Celtic in a July 2007 pre-season friendly.

Mark Viduka scores against West Ham in September 2007.

RIGHT: The new-look St James'
Park is just as impressive from the
outside as it is inside the stadium.

OPPOSITE: It's a far cry from the
packed ground in this mid-1950s
picture.

NORWICH CITY

Address:	Carrow Road, Norwich NR1 1JE
Website:	www.canaries.co.uk
Ground capacity:	26,034
Pitch dimensions:	105m x 67m
Opened:	1935
Premiership member:	1992-95, 2004-05
Record attendance:	43,984 v Leicester City, 30 March 1963, FA Cup

Opened in 1935, Carrow Road is home to Norwich City. The Club moved from the Nest on Rosary Road when the former ground could no longer adequately accommodate a League side. Carrow Road was the club's third home ground since their humble beginnings in 1902 and the first competitive match took place on 31 August 1935 when the home side won 4-3 against West Ham United.

Today, there are four stands at the stadium including the north east stand, the Barclay, the Norwich and Peterborough Stand in the south west, the Geoffrey Watling City Stand situated to the north west of the pitch and the Jarrold Stand which sits in the south east. The Barclay End was demolished in 1992 and a new structure consisting of two tiers was built modelled on the Norwich and Peterborough Stand. Named after Captain Evelyn Barclay, the club's former vice-president, it sits behind one of the goals where its supports a set of floodlights.

The Norwich and Peterborough Stand, originally called the River End due to its proximity to the River Wensum, was rebuilt in 1979 and named after its sponsor, the Norwich and Peterborough Building Society. The new construction consisted of a two tier replacement that cost £1.7 million. The Geoffrey Watling City Stand consists of a single tier and was renovated following a devastating fire in 1984. Originally known as the City Stand, the new construction was opened officially by the Duchess of Kent in 1987 and was named in honour of former president Geoffrey Watling who died in 2004. Here the directors' box, media and hospitality suites can be found and is joined at both ends to the Barclay End and the former River End. The last stand to be built at the stadium was the Jarrold Stand which was erected in 2003 when the South Stand was knocked down. The stand is sponsored by a local department store and, like the Geoffrey Watling Stand, is single tier. It was expanded to meet the Norwich and Peterborough Stand two years later.

Should the club, once again, find themselves in the Premiership, there are plans to increase the stadium's capacity. The Canaries have established themselves in recent years as a consistent Championship side but their only outing in the Premiership in the last ten years lasted just one campaign. That was the 2004-05 season when, after claiming the First Division title the previous year, they finished a disappointing nineteenth in the top flight, recording just seven wins in their 38 League games.

As well as hosting Norwich City matches, the ground has also been used by the England Under-21 team who have visited Carrow Road on three occasions. The England Under-19s have also played on the pitch as have the England women's team who first visited the stadium in 2002. They returned in 2006 to claim a 1-0 victory against Iceland.

The stadium has also hosted a number of rock and pop concerts. In 1997, Status Quo performed at Carrow Road. Other acts to have graced the arena include Sir Elton John, Lulu, Sophie Ellis Bexter and George Michael.

Although three of the ground's corners meet, the fourth corner has been occupied by a hotel between the Barclay End and the Jarrold Stand. Construction of the hotel began in 2006 and was opened the following year with pitch-view rooms overlooking the stadium.

Norwich entertain West Ham in February 2004.

OPPOSITE: The exterior of Carrow Road's Barclay End Stand.

LEFT: Norwich have called Carrow Road home since 1935.

Carrow Road now has a capacity of more than 26,000.

NOTTINGHAM FOREST

Address:	The City Ground, Nottingham NG2 5FJ
Website:	www.nottinghamforest.co.uk
Ground capacity:	30,602
Pitch dimensions:	102m x 68m
Opened:	1898
Premiership member:	1992-93, 1994-97, 1998-99
Record attendance:	49,946 v Manchester United, 28 October 1967, Division One

The City Ground, situated in West Bridgford in Nottinghamshire, is home to Nottingham Forest. Built on the banks of the River Trent, this 30,602 capacity stadium was first used by the club in 1898 when they moved from Trent Bridge and their former Town Ground. When Nottingham became a city in 1897, the current City Ground name was chosen to reflect the urban area's newly established status. At first, the ground was left open on three sides and, despite the lack of protection from the elements, it was considered one of the finest in the country having been prepared by J W Bardill. The club had the opportunity to buy the ground for £7,000 in the mid-1930s but this never materialized.

In 1957, at a cost of £40,000, a new East Stand was erected with bench seating for around 2,500 fans. The Busby Babes were the visitors at the grand opening where they defeated the home side 2-1 in front of a record crowd of 47,804. The ball was signed by both teams and is still kept in the Trophy Room today.

The Main Stand was rebuilt in 1965 but, sadly, was destroyed by fire three years later during a Division One game. Luckily, no one was hurt in the accident but many of the club's records and trophies were lost forever. The Executive Stand was erected in 1980 and later renamed the Brian Clough Stand with its executive boxes and hospitality suites. Then, in the early part of the following decade, further redevelopment was carried out on the Bridgford Stand. This incorporated an unusual shape to the roof (which allows sunlight to reach the houses behind in Colwick Road) as well as a management suite. The Trent End was rebuilt in time for Euro '96.

Should Nottingham Forest be promoted again to the Premiership there is room for further expansion which would take the capacity up to 46,000 if needs be. However, in the summer of 2007, the club announced that it may be looking to move to a new stadium (capacity 50,000) although relocation would not be planned until 2014.

The Nottingham Express Transit would serve the ground from the city centre and club officials are hopeful that a move would ensure Forest's ability to host matches for the World Cup in 2018 if England were successful in its bid to stage the prestigious event. However, fans have been sceptical about the news citing that the League club is hardly in a position to justify a brand new stadium.

The club argues that the current stands – in 10 years time for example – will need further updating and refurbishment which will all cost considerable amounts of money. Names for the new purpose-built stadium including the Brian Clough Arena, the Robin Hood Arena and the New City Ground have already been suggested. Despite their recent and dramatic fall from the top flight to the Football League Division One, the Forest board are confident that they will be back in the Premiership by the time a new stadium is completed.

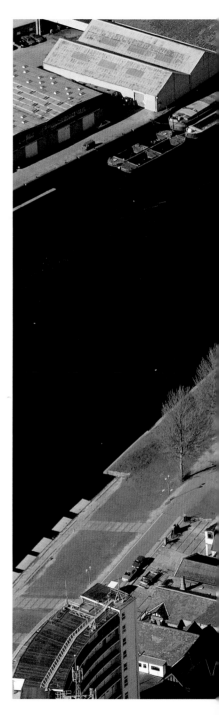

RIGHT: A ground fit for the Premiership, but Forest had slumped to the third tier of English football by the mid-2000s.

OPPOSITE: The City Ground has been home to Forest since 1898 and currently boasts a capacity of more than 30,000.

LEFT: Policemen attempt to stop the crowd encroaching onto the City Ground pitch in 1934.

OLDHAM ATHLETIC

Address:	Boundary Park, Furtherwood Road, Oldham OL1 2PA
Website:	www.oldhamathletic.co.uk
Ground capacity:	13,595
Pitch dimensions:	101m x 66m
Opened:	1907
Premiership member:	1992-94
Record attendance:	46,471 v Sheffield Wednesday, 25 January 1930, FA Cup

Bordering Chadderton and Royton in an area of Greater Manchester lies the aptly named Boundary Park, home to Oldham Athletic. The stadium also supports a number of other sporting activities and was built in 1904, the same year that it opened its doors. It is also home to Oldham Roughyeds RLFC who left their former ground, Watersheddings, in the latter part of the 1990s. The current capacity of the stadium is 13,595 and it was converted to an all-seater ground during the 1994-95 season following Oldham Athletic's relegation from the Premiership.

Renowned for being extremely cold, the stadium was given the nickname Ice Station Zebra. During the late 1990s, there was talk of moving the club to a new purpose-built ground on waste ground adjacent to Boundary Park, however, these plans were eventually abandoned. Development and change was still necessary though, and in February 2006, it was announced that the current site would undergo significant renovations in order to bring the stadium into the 21st century.

Apart from the Rochdale Road End – which is allocated to away supporters – the other three stands would be developed. In addition, the stadium's capacity would rise to 16,000 and a four star hotel along with conference and banqueting facilities would be established. Also included in the new plans were office space (totalling up to 100,000 square feet with apartments and leisure facilities which would house a fitness club and swimming pool. As a result of the proposals, the club were given planning permission in November 2007 to being work on the North Broadway Stand.

Situated on Sheepfoot Lane, Boundary Park hosts Oldham Athletic's home games. The club was formed in 1895 and was originally known as Pine Villa FC before changing its name in 1899. Oldham joined the Football League at the start of the 1907-08 season having established themselves at their current stadium some three years before. They were then promoted to the top flight a couple of years later. Despite their rise to Division One (as it was then), the club have never won any major trophies and their last appearances in the Premiership came between 1992 and 1994. The Latics were, in fact, one of the 22 founder members of the Premiership in the inaugural 1992-93 season.

But despite a lack of major silverware, the club have won three championships during their long history. They won the Second Division in the 1990-91 season and the Third Division twice; in 1952-53 and 1973-74.

There have been highs and lows at Oldham and in 2003 the club were forced into administration. Luckily, the club came to the attention of three US-based businessmen – Simon Blitz, Simon Corney and Danny Gazal – who purchased the club in November 2004. The most successful manager in the club's history must surely be Joe Royle who took charge between 1982 and 1994. Under Royle's guidance, the club achieved promotion and reached one League Cup final as well as two FA Cup semi-finals.

RIGHT: The Seton Stand can accommodate 3,600 people and cost £1.5 million to construct.

Oldham were one of the few clubs who installed an artificial playing surface in the 1980s but reverted to a grass pitch when they won promotion to the top flight.

*Mark Hughes outwits
Manchester City's Joey Barton
in January 2005.*

PORTSMOUTH

Address:	Fratton Park, Frogmore Road, Portsmouth PO4 8RA
Website:	www.pompeyfc.co.uk
Ground capacity:	20,688
Pitch dimensions:	100m x 65m
Opened:	1898
Premiership member:	2003-
Record attendance:	51,385 v Derby County, 26 February 1949, FA Cup

Fratton Park, also known fondly as Fortress Fratton, is the home stadium of Portsmouth with a current capacity of 20,688. The club plays on a 100 metre long and 65 metre wide grass pitch and has a long and established history with Fratton Park having moved there in 1898.

The Main Stand was designed by Archie Leitch, the Scottish architect who also built an ornate pavilion at the ground which is reminiscent of the similar building at Craven Cottage (home to Fulham). Sadly, much of this was removed when the ground was eventually expanded. All four of the stadium's stands are seated and the pitch runs from east to west.

The Fratton End is the ground's largest and most up-to-date stand. Standing opposite the Milton End in the west, the stand has the North and South Stands to either side (which both consist of two tiers). To the east of the pitch is the Milton End which is relatively small compared to the other three constructions. At one time, this more compact stand was the only roofless construction in the Premier League but it was brought more in line when a new roof was added for the start of the 2007-08 season. The Milton End is shared by both home and away supporters.

One particularly noticeable feature at Fratton Park is the mock Tudor façade at the original Fratton End entrance while many renovations have

taken place at the ground since the arrival of owner Alexandre Gaydamak. Today there are new and improved dressing rooms as well as a giant screen between the North Stand and the Milton End.

Unfortunately, due to the stadium's age and the length of time that Fratton Park has been home to Pompey (as the club is known) there are many signs of wear and tear and much of the ground falls short of the stadia used by other rival Premiership sides. Numerous suggestions have been made over the years as to how the club can improve facilities. As a result, initial plans included a move to a new stadium on a disused rail freight depot. Having gained city council approval the club changed their minds and decided to redevelop the existing site.

The new proposal included a "Pompey Village" which would contain housing, a hotel and retail outlets on surrounding land, as well as realigning the pitch by ninety degrees to allow for increased capacity. Work was due to begin in mid-2006 and the first new stands were scheduled to be ready for the start of the 2007-08 season.

Once again, however, the plans changed and a further announcement was made. This time, the plan was to build a new stadium, however, this time on a completely new site. The ambitious plan was to construct a 36,000 capacity ground on reclaimed mud flats near to the existing naval base. The proposals were grand in design and a huge leisure village was planned around the stadium. There would be more than 1,000 waterfront luxury apartments as well as restaurants and other facilities.

There was fairly widespread approval for the plans although some pointed out that the mud flats were close to a "Site of Special Scientific Interest". Again, the proposal fell through (in part due to the problems with access to the site) and a further set of plans were announced for building on reclaimed land at Horsey Island. For the time being, Portsmouth are to remain at Fratton Park where the faithful supporters can ring out the Pompey chimes.

There have been many suggestions put forward as to how Fratton Park can be expanded, including rotating the existing stadium by 90 degrees or moving to nearby Farlington.

RIGHT: *Jermain Defoe scores against Sunderland in February 2008.*

OPPOSITE: *A fog-bound Fratton Park before a clash with Chelsea in March 1997.*

OPPOSITE: *A newly-laid pitch awaits the finishing touches.*

LEFT: *Packed terraces in October 1948.*

QUEENS PARK RANGERS

Address:	Loftus Road Stadium, South Africa Road,
	Shepherds Bush, London W12 7PA
Website:	www.qpr.co.uk
Ground capacity:	18,420
Pitch dimensions:	101m x 67m
Opened:	1917
Premiership member:	1992-96
Record attendance:	35,353 v Leeds United,
	27 April 1974, Division One

The Blue Box, the Bush or Legoland are all names associated with Loftus Road in the west of London and home to Queens Park Rangers. The stadium was originally built in 1896 but didn't open until 1904 when it was the main ground for Shepherds Bush FC. The amateur side disbanded with the onset of the First World War and Queens Park Rangers moved to the site in 1917 from Park Royal Showground, their first football ground, although they did endure spells at White City in the 1930s and 1960s. The stadium is named after Robert Owen Loftus Versfeld who was instrumental in the club's early years. Having founded organized sporting events in South Africa, Versfeld set about encouraging the club into top flight football.

The Loftus Road End (also referred to as "the Loft") is not the only South African connection at Loftus Road. The South Africa Road Stand is often called Little South Africa and many of the roads surrounding the stadium have an association with the country. The two remaining stands comprise the Ellerslie Road Stand and the School End which accommodates away supporters.

The stadium claimed a first when it became the only ground in professional football to install an artificial pitch in 1981 (few other clubs

followed suit). However, it was removed seven years later and replaced with grass due to new footballing legislation.

The Loft sits behind the goal and consists of two tiers and is traditionally where members and season ticket holders can usually to be found. The Blue and White bar is popular while the stand itself is frequently sold out. The South Africa Road Stand and the Paddocks is the largest of the ground's four stands and is a two tier stand which also houses the dugouts, dressing rooms, administration offices, box office and the club shop. The Paddocks is the cheapest area in which to get a seat while the upper tier in the stand is the most expensive. The Ellerslie Road Stand is home for club sponsorship and as a result is often renamed. As a single tier stand it is the only one not painted in blue and white – for sponsorship reasons – and is a firm favourite with fans. The last construction, the School End, is a mirror image of the Loft.

The ground was also home to London Wasps (formerly known as Wasps RFC) between 1996 and 1997 and then again from 2001 to 2002 as part of a seven year ground-share deal devised by Wasps owner Chris Wright, at a time when rugby union was turning professional. However, when Fulham needed a ground to rent between 2002 and 2004 in order for redevelopment to take place at Craven Cottage, Wasps agreed to move to Adams Park, the home of Wycombe Wanderers. When London Wasps became infinitely successful following their somewhat enforced move they didn't return to Loftus Road despite Fulham's move back to their own stadium. As well as ground-sharing at various points, the stadium has also hosted a number of international friendly matches, the most recent of which was in November 2005 when Australia and Ghana enjoyed a 1-1 draw.

Having been a stalwart of the top flight since winning promotion in 1983, QPR were founder members of the Premiership in 1992 but suffered relegation in 1996.

Mikele Leigertwood scores in March 2008.

RIGHT: The exterior of Loftus Road.

OPPOSITE: An aerial view of Loftus Road, home to QPR since 1917 (apart from a couple of brief spells at White City in the 1930s and 1960s).

READING

Address:	Madejski Stadium, Junction 11, M4, Reading RG2 0FL
Website:	www.readingfc.co.uk
Ground capacity:	24,225
Pitch dimensions:	101m x 68m
Opened:	1998
Premiership member:	2006-
Record attendance:	24,374 v Blackburn Rovers, 29 March 2008, Premier League

Costing more than £50 million with its Desso GrassMaster pitch surface (mixed with real grass) and capacity for more than 24,000, the Madejski Stadium currently has two tenants, Reading FC and London Irish, the Rugby Union club. The stadium was opened on 22 August 1998 and Reading have made it their home ever since, however, London Irish didn't occupy the site until the beginning of the new millennium and for the first year of the stadium's life, Richmond FC agreed to ground-share with Reading. The stadium is also the finishing line of the Reading half marathon.

The inaugural match was held on that same day in the summer of 1998 when Reading beat Luton Town 3-0. Grant Brebner had the honour of scoring the stadium's first ever goal in an exciting match for the home side. The Madejski Stadium is built on a former dump (for household waste) situated close to the M4 motorway and is a bowl-styled venue surrounded by methane vents. Reading Borough Council sold the land to Reading FC for an astonishing £1.00 and the club named their new stadium after John Madejski, Reading's chairman. However, the ground is actually owned by the club.

Reading was promoted to the Premier League for the first time in their history at the start of the 2006-07 season. Due to increased interest in the performance of the club following their rise to the top flight, in October 2006 it was announced that a planning application would be submitted to increase the ground's capacity to around 38,000. This would be achieved by extending the East Stand with a further 6,000 seats which the North and South Stands would also undergo some development to reach the estimated (and desired) target.

The club made their application in January 2007 and the Council accepted the proposed changes and planning permission was granted at the end of May that same year. Work began on the expansion in the summer of 2008 to the East Stand. The North and South Stands would be redeveloped the following year.

The North Stand is the home stand while the South Stand is reserved for away fans with a current capacity of 2,327. However, when Reading reached the dizzy heights of the Premiership, it was decided that half the stand towards the East Stand would still be designated for the visiting side's fans, but that the other half would be used to accommodate ticket-only home supporters. The West Stand consists of two tiers and executive boxes are located between the upper and lower parts of the building. Here is where the tunnel and dugouts are located.

The highest attendance at the Madejski Stadium was recorded on 29 March 2008 when 24,374 fans turned out to watch Reading's match against Blackburn Rovers. Indeed, such has been the Royals' impact on the Premiership that they finished a more than creditable eighth in their first campaign. Also early in 2008, London Irish announced that it had signed a deal with Reading FC to remain tenants at the ground until 2026 due to the increase in crowd attendances at their home matches. On average, rugby matches at the stadium reach just over 11,000 while their record attendance was achieved in March 2007 when 22,648 spectators watched London Irish play Wasps.

Reading moved into the Madejski Stadium in 1998 and realised their ambition of Premiership football eight years later.

Reading's Kalifa Cisse clears off
the line against Manchester
United in January 2008.

Reading contest their first ever Premiership tie, against Middlesbrough, on 19 August 2006. It ended in a 3-2 victory for the home side.

SHEFFIELD UNITED

Address:	Bramall Lane Ground, Cherry Street,
	Bramall Lane, Sheffield S2 4SU
Website:	www.sufc.co.uk
Ground capacity:	32,609
Pitch dimensions:	101m x 68m
Opened:	1889
Premiership member:	2006-
Record attendance:	68,287 v Leeds United,
	15 February 1936, FA Cup

Bramall Lane is the oldest stadium in the world to still be hosting professional football. It was built on a road named after the Bramall family in 1855 and opened on 30 April in the Highfield area of Sheffield. The stadium is home to Sheffield United Football Club who made the ground their permanent home in 1889.

Originally the site opened as a cricket ground as part of a lease from the Duke of Norfolk and six clubs regularly played here managed by the Sheffield United Cricket Club. The first county match was held between Yorkshire and Sussex. Cricket remained prolific at the site and several records were made; in 1897, John Tunnicliffe and Jack Brown made a score of 378 (a ground record that has never been beaten). Maurice Leyland and his partnership with W Barber amassed an equally impressive score when they made 346 against Middlesex in 1932. But cricket at Bramall Lane came to an end in 1973, the South Stand was under construction and eventually the football pitch was enclosed on all four sides.

Today, the stadium has a capacity of 32,609, and became all-seater in 1994. The four main stands are joined by two corner stands in the north east and south west corners of the pitch. Currently, the south east corner remains open, although there are plans to fill it with seating when a leisure complex is added to the back of the South Stand. The Bramall Lane Stand is the oldest existing at the stadium and was opened in 1966 behind the goal at the Bramall Lane end. Since the 2006-07 season, the lower tier has been occupied by the visiting fans. Originally, the away fans occupied the upper tier and consequently had the best seats in the house, much to the annoyance of the home supporters.

The South Stand is also known as the Main Stand and was opened in 1975 (in fact, older supporters still refer to it as the "New Stand" due to its late-ish arrival at the stadium). The stand was renovated during the 2005-06 season and various sponsorships have followed. Most of the ground's facilities are located in the South Stand including the box office, a museum, a superstore and the award winning restaurant, 1889.

Opposite the South Stand lies the Kop which has consisted entirely of seating since 1991. The noise of the home fans from the Kop is so loud that Kevin Blackwell, the club's former assistant manager called it the "Bramall Roar". This is also the largest stand at the stadium. The John Street Stand is reserved for families only – completed in 1996, it can accommodate almost 7,000 spectators. Kop Corner, also known as the Northeast Corner or Evolution Corner was completed in 2001 while the Westfield Health stand is linked to the Bramall Lane Stand's upper tier. The Blades Business Centre occupies the north west corner of the ground offering office space to small and newly formed companies.

The Blades have endured a yo-yo existence in the League since their election in 1892. While they were founder members of the Premiership in 1992, their residency lasted just two seasons and it would take them until 2006 before they again graced the top flight. This time, they made an immediate return to the Championship but could not find the sustained form to mount a serious promotion challenge.

RIGHT: Bramall Lane in December 1999.

LEFT: Bramall Lane is snowed
under in March 2006.

ABOVE: The Blades score their
second goal against West Ham in
April 2007.

LEFT: Bramall Lane has been home to Sheffield United since 1889.

OPPOSITE: Brazilian legend Pelé visits Bramall Lane in November 2007 to celebrate the 150th anniversary of the world's oldest football club as Sheffield FC play Inter Primavera.

SHEFFIELD WEDNESDAY

Address:	Hillsborough, Sheffield S6 1SW
Website:	www.swfc.co.uk
Ground capacity:	39,814
Pitch dimensions:	106m x 65m
Opened:	1899
Premiership member:	1992-2000
Record attendance:	72,841 Manchester City, 17 February 1934, FA Cup

Located in the Owlerton area of Sheffield, Hillsborough Stadium was opened in September 1899 and Sheffield Wednesday have had their permanent home here since that time. Sadly, the stadium is synonymous with one of football's most tragic events when 96 Liverpool fans were crushed to death in an FA Cup semi-final match between Liverpool and Nottingham Forest in April 1989. The horrific circumstances would lead to major reforms in football stadiums across the country and the Taylor Report – set up specifically following that fateful day – recommended that all terracing was converted to all-seater accommodation. There is a memorial to all those who lost their lives near the ground's main entrance on Parkside Road.

As a result of the tragedy, and in line with new legislation, Hillsborough is now a 39,814 capacity all-seater stadium and, despite little investment or renovations since the mid-1990s, is still considered to be a fantastic ground with its two grand, two tiered stands and two large single tiered stands and its one filled corner known as the North West Terrace.

The site at Owlerton was offered to the club when they were required to move from their former ground at Olive Grove. Originally known as the Owlerton Stadium, Hillsborough became the ground's new name in 1912

which came from the newly formed parliamentary constituency in the area. The first eight years of the club's time at Hillsborough have proved to have been their best to-date, and they claimed their first League titles during the 1902-03 campaign and then again the following season. Following the end of the Second World War, the stadium was among the top grounds in the country and went on to host a total of twenty seven FA Cup semi-finals. It was also chosen as a venue for the 1966 World Cup following some renovations of the earlier stands.

Further renovations came in the mid-1990s in time for Euro '96 and Sheffield Wednesday played host, in particular, to the Danish squad. A year later and Hillsborough hosted its first major match since the disaster in 1989 when the League Cup final replay took place between Leicester City and Middlesbrough. However, Hillsborough would suffer more problems in 2007 when the River Don burst its banks. Many parts of Sheffield were affected by severe flash flooding, prolonged rainfall and inadequate drainage and soak-aways. In June 2007, the pitch, dressing rooms, restaurants, kitchens and boardroom were all flooded under several feet of water. The box office, superstore, alongside many local residents in nearby housing were also affected and the clean-up operation was immense.

Today, the West Stand that was constructed at the turn of the 20th century has a seating capacity of 7,995 and is situated at the Leppings Lane End of the ground while the original South Stand came from Olive Grove and was rebuilt at the Owlerton site in 1899. The clock face on the South Stand is still the original. The Spion Kop was built in 1914 and is referred to by fans as the Kop. Situated to the east end of the stadium, it has a current seating capacity of 11,210.

RIGHT: Hillsborough pictured in 1996, after it was chosen as one of the venues for Euro '96.

RIGHT: *Sheffield Wednesday and Sunderland observe a minute's silence in September 2001.*

OPPOSITE: *Hillsborough in 2000, the last year that Wednesday graced the Premiership.*

Hillsborough – known as Owlerton before 1912 – has been the Owls' home since 1899.

Hillsborough has a capacity of almost 40,000.

SOUTHAMPTON

Address:	St Mary's Stadium, Britannia Road, Southampton SO14 5FP
Website:	www.saintsfc.co.uk
Ground capacity:	32,689
Pitch dimensions:	102m x 66m
Opened:	2001
Premiership member:	1992-2005
Record attendance:	32,104 v Liverpool, 18 January 2003, Premier League

The Dell, situated on Milton Road in Southampton, was home to the Saints between 1898 and 2001. The inaugural match took place on 3 September 1898 against Brighton United and the Saints claimed their first victory on home soil in a 4-1 win. Redevelopment of the site, bought by local fish merchant George Thomas, began in 1927 and the West Stand was demolished and replaced to a design by Archie Leitch. A fire broke out in the East Stand a year later and its replacement was built to mirror the West Stand while overall capacity was increased to around 30,000 spectators.

The Second World War would further complicate the ground when a German bomb left an 18 foot crater in the penalty area in November 1940 and the pitch had to be restored. The following year, in March, munitions that were stored at the stadium exploded causing yet another major fire – this time in the West Stand and it was rebuilt for a second time. The Dell was the first English football ground to have floodlights installed in 1950. The record attendance came on 8 October 1969 when 31,044 fans watched Manchester United (with Bobby Charlton and George Best) hammer the Saints in a 3-0 victory. Redevelopment occurred in the 1980s and capacity dropped to around 15,000 when the stadium became all-seater. By the 1990s, however, the Saints were looking for an alternative ground and the final match, fittingly, was against Brighton and Hove Albion on 26 May 2001.

The club's new site St Mary's Stadium (officially called the Friends Provident St Mary's Stadium) was opened in August 2001 about one and a half miles from the Dell on a disused gasworks. Construction began in 1999 for the 32,689 capacity ground. It is bowl-shaped with two enormous screens at either end of the stadium visible from any seat in the house. The four stands are named after the areas in the city that they overlook and comprise the main (east) stand, the Itchen, the Kingland Stand, the Chapel Stand and the Northam Stand to the north of the pitch. A translucent panel sits behind all but the Itchen stand and allows natural light to infiltrate the pitch while a large section of the Chapel Stand roof is also translucent for this very reason.

The club faced some controversy over an eleven foot statue of former club president Ted Bates which was unveiled on 17 March 2007. Made by sculptor Ian Brennan, the statue was condemned for its less than accurate portrayal of the Saints' stalwart and it was removed less than a week after it was erected and negotiations are ongoing about how to rectify the situation.

As well as the action on the pitch, St Mary's also offers a number of facilities for other uses. It is a fully-functioning conference facility and the Saints Study Support Centre is a club run to help local school children from the Northam stand. The stadium has also hosted a number of film premiers including *Casino Royale* and music concerts where notable artists to perform here include Bon Jovi, Craig David and Sir Elton John.

RIGHT: Kenwyne Jones celebrates scoring at St Mary's Stadium in May 2007.

OPPOSITE: St Mary's Stadium in 2001-02, its inaugural season.

LEFT: St Mary's boasts a capacity of more than 32,500.

Referee Howard Webb waits as the game between Southampton and Manchester United is disrupted by a firework being thrown onto the pitch in March 2005.

The Dell was home to Southampton for more than 100 years before the club's move in 2001.

SUNDERLAND

Address:	Stadium of Light, Sunderland SR5 1SU
Website:	www.safc.com
Ground capacity:	49,000
Pitch dimensions:	105m x 68m
Opened:	1997
Premiership member:	1996-97, 1999-2003, 2005-06, 2007-
Record attendance:	48,353 v Liverpool, 13 April 2002, Premier League

Based in Sunderland in the north east of England is the Stadium of Light, home to Sunderland AFC. The 49,000 capacity ground came about when Roker Park, the club's former stadium, was going to prove too costly and too difficult to convert from a virtually all standing terraced footballing arena into a completely seated venue. Having abandoned initial plans, the club found the former site of Wearmouth Colliery the perfect solution in 1995. Located on the north bank of the River Wear in Sheepfolds, the ground was just a stone's throw from Roker Park and it was announced in November that year that the Tyne and Wear Development Corporation (TWDC) had given their approval. Costing a total of £34 million the Stadium of Light was opened in 1997.

The stadium's name was chosen via a competition and was revealed to mixed reactions. To reflect the fact that many fans would have worked in the Sunderland mines, light was an important consideration and a giant Davy lamp (the miners' safety lamp created and developed by the Cornish chemist and physicist Sir Humphry Davy) was erected in front of the box office.

The four stands are named after the four points on the compass and the West Stand also comprises the Premier Concourse (the upper tier) and executive boxes. This is also where the main entrance to the stadium is found along with the players' dressing rooms, the tunnel, hospitality and banqueting suites, media facilities and the sports bar. The pitch itself is several metres below the level of ground surrounding the stadium. The stadium has a concourse that runs right the way around the pitch except for the away supporters' area which remains separate. Away supporters are generally seated in the South Stand while the North Stand is often referred to as the home end.

In contrast to the glitz of the Stadium of Light, Roker Park was considered "tired" when Sunderland finally moved from the ground in 1997. It had been the club's faithful home for almost 100 years (the ground was opened in 1898) and was situated to the north of the city. Originally, Sunderland had played at Newcastle Road, but the then chairman decided a new and improved ground was a prerequisite. He bought a piece of land in Roker (hence the name) and it was officially opened by Charles Vane-Tempest-Stewart, the Marquess of Londonderry, having been designed by Archie Leitch. The inaugural match saw the home side win 1-0 (with a Jim Leslie goal) against Liverpool. The first floodlights in 1952 were temporary and were replaced by more permanent structures at the end of the season following their unprecedented success.

The ground was a host venue for the 1966 World Cup and improvements were assured. Further renovations were carried out during the 1970s but the following decade saw a downturn in the club's fortunes. Existing within a highly-populated area meant that expansion at Roker Park would be nigh on impossible. Added to which, converting the stadium to all-seater would drastically reduce capacity and, in turn, the club's revenue. Hence the move to the Stadium of Light seemed an inevitable conclusion although Sunderland share the dubious distinction (with Crystal Palace) of having spent four separate spells in the Premiership. The Black Cats also registered the lowest ever points total (15) in 2005-06.

The Stadium of Light is located in a picturesque setting in Sunderland

LEFT: The Stadium of Light has witnessed two relegations from the Premiership as well as three promotions to the top flight.

OPPOSITE: *Sunderland have to battle the elements as well as their opponents Fulham in their attempt to avoid relegation in April 2006.*

LEFT: *Mounted police patrol outside the Fulwell End of Roker Park in March 1997.*

SWINDON TOWN

Address:	County Ground, County Road, Swindon SN1 2ED
Website:	www.swindontownfc.co.uk
Ground capacity:	14,800
Pitch dimensions:	101m x 69m
Opened:	1896
Premiership member:	1993-94
Record attendance:	32,000 v Arsenal, 15 January 1972, FA Cup

Located close to the town of Swindon, is the County Ground, the home of Swindon Town Football Club. The site first opened its doors in 1896 and has remained the club's permanent base for more than 100 years.

Prior to playing at County Ground, Swindon Town were based at the adjacent cricket pitch (also called County Ground) for three years. Originally known as Wiltshire County Ground, the new site received £300 from Arkell's Brewery, in order to finance the building of a stand. However, like a great many other stadiums, war stopped play and, during the early 1940s, prisoners of war were housed in huts on the pitch. Eventually the POWs moved out, the club was compensated and floodlights were an additional bonus for players and fans alike in 1951. Installed at a cost of £350, the new lights gave Swindon Town the honour of being the first League Club to have them. The North Stand (also known as Arkell's) was built in 1971 and the stadium became all-seater during the early 1990s.

Today, the ground is owned by Swindon Borough Council and while a move to a stadium owned by the club has been considered, funding has remained an issue. Seemingly set to stay at the County Ground, the club undertook a massive redevelopment campaign in order to update the somewhat outdated facilities by raising a petition with the Council in 2006. Future plans in the ground's renovations include improving the playing surface.

The four stands include the aforementioned Arkell's along with Stratton Bank, Town End and Kingswood Stand. Located at the east end of the pitch, Stratton Bank remains uncovered despite planning permission to build one. Some away supporters are accommodated here when the size of the crowed necessitates it. Otherwise, the stand is home to Swindon Town supporters who are seated below the scoreboard. Opposite Arkell's sits Town End (named for its proximity to Swindon itself) which is particularly popular with the club's more vocal fans.

Kingswood Stand is situated at the south end of the pitch and was built in the early 1990s. Sponsored by Kingswood, it was originally named the Intel Stand and was sponsored by Nationwide. However, fans are known to refer to it as the South Stand and it remains a firm favourite with its cantilever roof. Finally, Arkell's is named after the brewery founded by Thomas Arkell who was instrumental in the original stand's construction. The stand lies opposite the Kingswood Stand to the north and sports large windshields. It is here that executive seating, the tunnel, a VIP lounge and the players' dressing rooms are found. The west corner of Arkell's is reserved for away fans and new red and white seating will be added imminently to give the stand a more up-to-date look.

As well as playing host to Swindon Town's home matches, the ground has also been used for women's international games, England Under-17s, community football and local schools competitions as well as rock and pop concerts for the likes of Sir Elton John and Bryan Adams.

RIGHT: Dark clouds gather over the County Ground in January 2008.

RIGHT: The County Ground hosted Premiership football for just one season, the 1993-94 campaign.

TOTTENHAM HOTSPUR

Address:	White Hart Lane, Bill Nicholson Way, 748 High Road, Tottenham, London N17 0AP
Website:	www.tottenhamhotspur.co.uk
Ground capacity:	36,310
Pitch dimensions:	100m x 67m
Opened:	1899
Premiership member:	1992-
Record attendance:	75,038 v Sunderland, 5 March 1938, FA Cup

Often referred to as "the Lane" or "WHL", White Hart Lane in north London is the home of Tottenham Hotspur. In fact, the club moved to their present site in 1899 after spells at Tottenham Marshes and Northumberland Park and their inaugural match against Notts County saw the home side claim a 4-1 victory when the ground opened in September that year. More than 5,000 spectators witnessed Spurs' first game – in the then Division One – which brought the club an income of £115 through ticket sales. Encouragingly, 11,000 fans turned up on 9 September 1899 for the club's first competitive fixture five days later when Queens Park Rangers were defeated 1-0 at the stadium.

By 1904, White Hart Lane had been honoured with its first stand which boasted seating for 500 and there were plans to buy the ground outright. Shares costing £1.00 each were sold through the club handbook in order to raise the necessary £8,900 to purchase the freehold while further monies were needed to buy land at the Edmonton End. As a result of the shares bought in this way, the club was able to establish a huge bank at the Paxton Road End in a mirror image of the bank at the opposite Park Lane End. By this time, the overall capacity at White Hart Lane had reached a healthy 40,000.

With their roots firmly established in the Football League, Archie Leitch was hired to design a new Main Stand. His finished plans included a capacity of 5,300 seated and 6,000 standing, completed in 1909 in time for a Division One match against Manchester United in September. Also that year, the East Stand was given a roof while a copper cockerel was added to the apex of the mock-Tudor gable. In 1911, the East Stand was further developed and brought the ground's capacity up to 50,000. However, by 1934, the ground's further renovations and redevelopment (again, with designs by Leitch) meant this had been dramatically increased to almost 80,000.

Floodlights were introduced in 1953 and little development took place at White Hart Lane until the early 1970s. Spurs were, by now, firmly ensconced as one of the top flight clubs and were regularly enjoying large crowds of spectators. During the early 1980s, the West Stand was built under poor management which resulted in delayed completion that eventually brought about severe financial implications. The three tier East Stand (which today has a total capacity of 10,691) originally had a standing terrace on the middle tier which offered extremely good views of the pitch. This section was fondly known by fans as "the Shelf", however, renovations and legislation made the tier all-seater in the early 1990s. Sadly, although fairly modern in design, the lack of cantilever roof on the East Stand and the roof supports that obstruct view in certain seats marks the construction's true age.

The South Stand didn't appear until the start of the 1990s. Located on the Park Lane End, the stand was designed with a giant video screen (there are now two) and renovation to the North Stand was completed just before the new millennium. As home matches continue to draw huge crowds, there are rumours of Spurs relocating to a large purpose-built stadium, however, the club look set to continue at White Hart Lane for the foreseeable future.

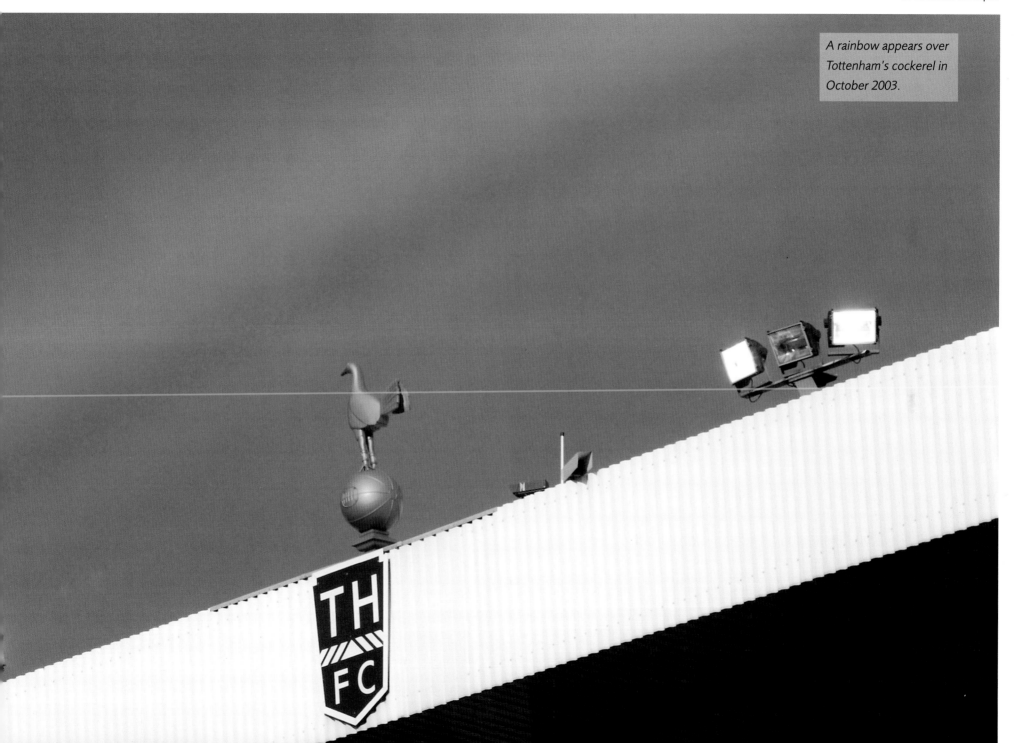

A rainbow appears over Tottenham's cockerel in October 2003.

OPPOSITE: White Hart Lane as Spurs take on Aston Villa in October 2007.

LEFT: An aerial view of White Hart Lane in September 2006.

RIGHT: Darren Bent scores against West Ham in March 2008.

OPPOSITE: Tottenham entertain Everton during the 2003-04 campaign.

The White Hart Lane capacity now stands at more than 36,000.

The Tottenham Hotspur groundstaff, managers, trainers and players line up together in front of the West Stand for a group photograph in 1950.

WATFORD

Address:	Vicarage Road Stadium, Vicarage Road, Watford WD18 0ER
Website:	www.watfordfc.com
Ground capacity:	19,920
Pitch dimensions:	105m x 69m
Opened:	1922
Premiership member:	1999-2000, 2006-07
Record attendance:	34,099 v Manchester United, 3 February 1969, FA Cup

Built in 1922, Vicarage Road was opened on 30 August, that same year. Home to Watford Football Club and Saracens Rugby Club, the ground has a current capacity of 19,920. Prior to moving to Vicarage Road, Watford were based on Cassion Road in the town of Watford. The inaugural match was against Millwall on 30 August 1922. The first stand to be constructed at the stadium was the Vicarage Road Stand at the end of the 1922-23 season. It was initially an earth bank, but gradually over time, was replaced with open terracing. In 1978, an electric scoreboard was a welcome addition to the stand and it became synonymous with Watford's heyday in the 1980s.

However, renovations in the early 1990s ensured that the stand was brought in line to comply with the Taylor Report at a cost of £2.3 million. Today, it has a capacity of 5,800 and is, of course, all seater. The new stand was opened for a match against Notts County on 18 September 1993 where the home side won 3-1. It is now the stand occupied by away supporters on match days (although it was a home stand up until 1999). Then, in 2004, it was decided to partition the stand so that home and away fans could both use the stand. Running alongside the west of the pitch is the Rous Stand, named after former FIFA president Sir Stanley Rous. It was

built in 1986 replacing the Shrodells Stand and cost the club £3 million in development which was partly funded by a loan from Watford fanatic Sir Elton John. The stand consists of two tiers and the upper is complete with executive boxes. The Shrodells Stand (built in the 1930s) was preceded by the Union Stand which had originally come from Cassion Road. The stand was painstakingly taken down, transported and rebuilt at Vicarage Road when the club moved here in 1922.

The Main Stand was also built in 1922 and is located on the east side of the ground. Here the players' dressing rooms, tunnel, media area and directors' box is to be found while a section originates from the club's early days and is the oldest part of the stand still remaining. Benskins Breweries helped fund the original Main Stand – and also gave the club a 21 year lease on the land – but a new extension was added in 1969 and eventually a family enclosure was incorporated into the terrace.

The Rookery Stand is renowned for its upbeat (and noisy) atmosphere. It is currently the newest part of the stadium at Vicarage Road and was built during the 1994-95 season. Originally a terraced stand, it is now all-seater and has facilities which include the club shop and offices. The Rookery Stand was first opened to supporters in 1995 and has a capacity of 6,960.

When Watford underwent severe financial difficulties in 2002 the ground was temporarily sold. However, a campaign, "Let's Buy Back The Vic", ensured that the club was able to purchase their permanent home for £7.6 million in 2005. Watford's former owner, Sir Elton John, donated the entire proceeds of a performance at the ground for this very purpose. Unfortunately, the Hornets' two spells in the Premiership have seen them relegated at the first opportunity.

RIGHT: Vicarage Road prepares to host a relegation battle between Watford and Charlton Athletic in March 2007. As it turned out, neither side could avoid the drop at the end of the campaign.

RIGHT: Vicarage Road, home to the Hornets since 1922, now boasts a near-20,000 capacity.

OPPOSITE: A waterlogged pitch postponed Watford's Premiership match against Wigan Athletic in December 2006.

WEST BROMWICH ALBION

Address:	The Hawthorns, West Bromwich B71 4LF
Website:	www.wbafc.co.uk
Ground capacity:	28,003
Pitch dimensions:	105m x 68m
Opened:	1900
Premiership member:	2002-03, 2004-06
Record attendance:	64,815 v Arsenal, 6 March 1937, FA Cup

Since 1900 – when it was finally completed – the Hawthorns has been home to West Bromwich Albion. It has an unusual honour in being the highest of all Premiership grounds today at an altitude of 551 feet (168 metres). With its capacity of 28,003 it is the twenty-eighth largest stadium in English football.

Like a number of other clubs, West Brom had a fairly nomadic existence in its early days. There were five previous grounds associated with the club before it finally settled at the Hawthorns. These included Coopers Hill (their first ground), Dartmouth Park, Bunns Field, West Bromwich Dartmouth Cricket Club and Stoney Lane. Opened in September 1900, the Hawthorns first became an option for the club when their lease at Stoney Lane expired. It was the first time that they had moved to a site further away from the town of West Bromwich and the land was literally covered in hawthorn bushes. A lease for the land was signed in May 1900 with Sandwell Park Colliery and the club went on to purchase the freehold to the ground in 1913.

A 1-1 draw was the result of Albion's inaugural match against Derby County in September 1900 on a ground which was also used for athletics. The Hawthorns was the finishing line for the first marathon to be run in the Midlands by the Birchfield Harriers during the club's early years at the ground, while the first international match came on 21 October 1922 between England and Ireland resulting in a 2-0 home victory. The second international took place two years later when England again triumphed, this time over Belgium in a 4-0 win. By the early 1920s, concrete terracing had been built and floodlights followed several decades later in the latter half of the 1950s. When the Taylor Report was published, both the Smethwick End and the Birmingham Road End were demolished and replaced with all-seater stands, and in 2001 the Rainbow Stand was replaced by the new East Stand.

The Halfords Lane Stand (the West Stand) was built between 1979 and 1981 and was home to executive seating before the new East Stand was constructed. Here the media and press are found in the 5,110 capacity all-seater stand. The East Stand (completed in 2001) has a capacity for 10,000 spectators and houses the administration offices, club shop, box office and corporate entertainment suites. The two sides of the stand are called the Millennium Corner and the Woodman Corner. The Birmingham Road End which is joined to the Woodman Corner is better known as Brummie Road. Constructed in the mid-1990s, this stand has an overall capacity of 6,000. The Smethwick End seems to have become a firm favourite with fans and runs behind the goal at the south end of the pitch. Away fans are accommodated in part of the Smethwick End. Also built in the mid-1990s, it has a slightly lower capacity than the Birmingham Road End of 5,816.

Giant video screens were installed in 2002 and the following year saw the introduction of the Jeff Astle gates at the Birmingham Road End to commemorate one of the club's most prolific strikers. Also in 2003, it was announced that the club intended to increase the capacity to 40,000 although these plans have yet to materialize. It is likely that these proposals will be shelved until such time as Albion re-establish themselves back in the Premiership (they were relegated in 2006).

OPPOSITE: Flowers and scarves are laid in tribute to Jeff Astle in January 2002.

LEFT: The Hawthorns has seen much redevelopment over the years and now holds almost 28,000 spectators.

WEST HAM UNITED

Address:	The Boleyn Ground, Upton Park, Green Street, London E13 9AZ
Website:	www.whufc.co.uk
Ground capacity:	35,300
Pitch dimensions:	101m x 67m
Opened:	1904
Premiership member:	1993-2003, 2005-
Record attendance:	42,322 v Tottenham Hotspur, 17 October 1970, Division One

The Boleyn Ground, opened in 1904, is known by a variety of names including the Foundry, the Castle, Green Street and Mean Street, however, its most popular name must surely be Upton Park, based on the site's location. Home to West Ham United, Upton Park was the piece of land which the club decided to rent from an east London district. However, at the time, the land was actually part of Essex (and did not become part of London until 1965). The various names come about because of the land's association with Green Street House – once a school – which was known among locals as Boleyn Castle as it was said that wife of Henry VIII, Anne Boleyn, had once owned the house.

Like many other Premiership grounds, particularly in London and other large cities, Upton Park was affected by the Second World War. In August 1944, a bomb landed on the south west corner of the pitch advocating a move for the club while repairs were carried out. After meeting the new regulations during the 1990s following the Taylor Report, the stadium became all-seater and the four stands today comprise the East Stand, the Dr Martens Stand, the Bobby Moore Stand and the Centenary Stand. The latter was formerly known as the North Bank and was built in 1995 to mark West Ham's 100th season; the club was formed in 1895 under the name

Thames Ironworks. Today, the stand has a capacity of 6,000 on two tiers – the upper of which is generally reserved for families – while the lower tier is allocated to both home and away fans.

The Centenary stand is particularly popular with vocal West Ham supporters who prefer to stand and sing their way through matches. Situated in the corner of the Centenary and East Stands are two large LCD screens. The East Stand is the oldest and smallest in the stadium and was built in 1969. It is particularly narrow in width and holds a maximum of 5,000 supporters. Unusually, the stand still has some wooden seating left in the middle of the upper tier. The Bobby Moore Stand (known formerly as the South Bank) was built in 1993 to comply with all-seater regulations and today has a capacity of 9,000. When the legendary former club captain Bobby Moore died it was decided to rename the stand in his honour. There are executive boxes in both the upper and lower tiers.

The Dr Martens Stand holds 15,000 spectators and is by far the longest (and newest) stand within the stadium. It was built in 2001 and on completion gave the ground a total capacity of 35,647. Considered the main stand at Upton Park, Dr Martens Stand consists of two tiers separated by executive boxes. It also houses the club's administration offices, players' dressing rooms, club shop, museum, executive suites and the West Ham United Hotel. It is the largest single football stand of any stadium in London and two large turrets with the club's badge embedded on them are a striking feature from outside the ground.

There were plans to increase the ground's capacity to 40,500 by building a new, larger, East Stand, but relegation in 2003 put the proposal on hold for the time being. The Hammers' absence from the Premiership lasted only two seasons, however, and they have flourished since rejoining the top flight. Then, in November 2007, it was announced that a new site had been identified for a new stadium. West Ham fans would just have to wait and see what the future would bring.

Captured in duplicate – in case you're not sure, this is the home of West Ham United.

RIGHT: Prince Harry takes a penalty kick in front of youth squad members in September 2002.

OPPOSITE: Although more commonly known as Upton Park, West Ham's ground is actually named the Boleyn Ground after a house which stood near the site until the mid-20th century.

OPPOSITE: West Ham entertain Middlesbrough in October 2005.

LEFT: The club's home since 1904, Upton Park holds more than 35,000 fans.

WIGAN ATHLETIC

Address:	JJB Stadium, Robin Park, Newtown, Wigan WN5 0UZ
Website:	www.wiganathletic.tv
Ground capacity:	25,138
Pitch dimensions:	105m x 68m
Opened:	1999
Premiership member:	2005-
Record attendance:	25,023 v Liverpool, 11 February 2006, Premier League

The JJB, as it is often known, was built and opened in 1999. Located in the Robin Park Complex in Wigan, Greater Manchester, it is the stadium of Wigan Athletic Football Club and the Wigan Warriors Rugby League Club. Prior to moving to JJB, Wigan Athletic's home had been Springfield Park. The Club had spent 102 years at the stadium and prior to 1932 were known as Wigan Borough. Named after its principal sponsor, the JJB Stadium is owned by David Whelan (a former chairman of JJB). With a capacity of 25,138, it is an all-seater ground with structured terracing and a cantilevered steel roof with rectangular stands and open corners.

All away supporters, for both football matches and rugby, are allocated seats in the North Stand which sits behind the goal. The pitch, measuring 105 metres in length and 68 metres in width is a sand-based matrix containing an irrigation and undersoil heating system. Made of grass, the pitch also has around two percent of synthetic fibres which helps to stabilize the playing surface. Built by construction company Alfred McAlpine, the stadium was completed in August 1999.

The first match on the pitch was a friendly against Morecambe. However, in another friendly against local rivals Manchester United, Sir Alex Ferguson officially opened the JJB Stadium. The first competitive match took place later that same month on 7 August 1999 against Scunthorpe in Division Two. The home side were rewarded with a 3-0 victory at their inaugural game with Simon Haworth scoring twice, marking the stadium's first competitive goal.

In a surprise twist of fate, Wigan Athletic were also the first "away" team (with a brace from Stuart Barlow) to win at the JJB Stadium. Cambridge City's ground was deemed unsuitable for an FA Cup tie and Wigan used the away dressing rooms and wore their away strip in what was officially Cambridge's "home" game.

However, Wigan Warriors didn't fare as well as their football counterparts and lost their first game at the stadium on 19 September 1999 against Castleford Tigers. However, their fighting form returned in 2001 and they have had a great deal of success at their "new" home from that point on.

The success of both teams was somewhat blighted in 2005, however, when the Greater Manchester police announced that they would no longer police events at the stadium. A continuing row between owner David Whelan and the police over unpaid policing bills amounting to £300,000 were the issue. Although it would not have affected the Warriors unduly as rugby matches are overseen by stewards rather than the police, Wigan Athletic would have suffered had the stadium's safety certificate been revoked. An agreement was reached allowing the Premier team to continue playing to the end of the season and since then – wanting to avoid playing to an empty stadium – the debt was settled. However, the club immediately began an appeal with regard to the monies owed.

RIGHT: Wigan Athletic joined the Premiership in 2005 – 27 years after gaining initial Football League status – and have confounded their critics who claimed their stay would last just one campaign.

RIGHT: Wigan left their previous
Springfield Park ground and
moved to the JJB Stadium in 1999.

WOLVERHAMPTON WANDERERS

Address:	Molineux, Waterloo Road,
	Wolverhampton WV1 4QR
Website:	www.wolves.co.uk
Ground capacity:	28,576
Pitch dimensions:	101m x 69m
Opened:	1889
Premiership member:	2003-04
Record attendance:	61,315 v Liverpool,
	11 February 1939, FA Cup

Wolverhampton Wanderers have been in residence ever since the Molineux Stadium opened in 1889. The ground is situated within a mile of the city centre and much of the stadium is painted in gold (in line with the club's colors). Due to its sheer size, the stadium is a prominent landmark on the city's skyline. The four stands comprise the Steve Bull Stand (formerly named after John Ireland) which heralds the club's most prolific goal scorer, the Jack Harris Stand, the Stan Cullis Stand (former player, captain and manager) and the Billy Wright Stand (former Wolves and England player).

Today, the overall capacity of the stadium is 28,576. Having been increased in 2003 by building a temporary stand (the Graham Hughes Stand) for around 900 fans, the seating was removed for the start of the 2006-07 season to give the current number of allocated seats. However, prior to the Taylor Report the record attendance was 61,315 when Wolves entertained Liverpool in an FA Cup tie on 11 February 1939.

Local merchant, Benjamin Molineux purchased a plot of land in the city in 1744 on which to build his home. Molineux House, as it was known, later became the Molineux Hotel and the estate eventually changed hands in 1860 and a pleasure park was established as Molineux Grounds. Originally

there was a cycle track, ice rink, boating lake and football arena but the land was sold to Northampton Brewery in 1889 who rented it to Wolverhampton Wanderers (who had relied on a nomadic existence for some time). Having called Windmill Field, John Harper's Field and Dudley Road home, the Club bought the freehold to the land in 1923 and built a huge stand on the Waterloo Road side. This was followed by a further stand on the Molineux Street side and – with two further stands – the stadium was set for the next 50 years. Floodlights were installed in 1953 and in 1957 the club were ready to host their first European Cup games.

In 1975, the Molineux Street side had to be demolished and rebuilt due to safety concerns and the John Ireland Stand, as it was named, was opened four years later. However, despite the new impressive stand, the pitch remained where it was (the stand had been erected behind the old one) and the John Ireland Stand was some 100 feet from the touchline. Development had cost the club dearly and it was to prove one of the most expensive in the history of football stadia resulting in Wolves narrowly avoiding bankruptcy in the early 1980s.

By the middle of the decade, two stands – the North Bank and the Waterloo Road – were too dilapidated to accommodate spectators and the club's financial situation meant that the stadium became like a ruin. Wolverhampton Council purchased the ground in 1986, but the takeover of the club by Sir Jack Hayward in 1990 brought about Wolves' fortunes when redevelopment was planned. The Taylor Report ensured that the much-needed proposals were implemented and the newly renovated Molineux Stadium was opened on 7 December 1993.

It was Sir Jack's dream that Wolves be reunited with the top flight and while this happened in 2003, it was to last just one season.

RIGHT: A giant of yesteryear, Wolves failed to capitalize on their hard-earned promotion and spent just one season in the Premiership.

Left: Molineux, the club's home since 1889, was redeveloped at the end of the 20th century at a cost of more than £25 million.

PHOTO CREDITS